The Autism Checklist

The Autism Checklist

A Practical Reference for Parents and Teachers

Paula Kluth
with John Shouse

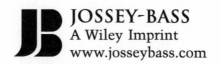

JOSSEY-BASS
A Wiley Imprint
www.josseybass.com

Published by Jossey-Bass
A Wiley Imprint
989 Market Street, San Francisco, CA 94103-1741—www.josseybass.com

Jossey-Bass books and products are available through most bookstores. To contact Jossey-Bass directly call our Customer Care Department within the U.S. at 800-956-7739, outside the U.S. at 317-572-3986, or fax 317-572-4002.

Jossey-Bass also publishes its books in a variety of electronic formats. Some content that appears in print may not be available in electronic books.

Library of Congress Cataloging-in-Publication Data

Kluth, Paula.
   The autism checklist : a practical reference for parents and teachers / Paula Kluth John Shouse.—1st ed.
      p. cm.
   Includes bibliographical references and index.
   ISBN 978-0-470-43408-6 (pbk.)
   1. Autistic children—Education—United States.   2. Autistic youth—Education—United States.   3. Home and school—United States.   I. Shouse, John. II. Title.
   LC4718.K573 2009
   371.94—dc22

                                                                        2009021543

Printed in the United States of America

FIRST EDITION

PB Printing   10 9 8 7 6 5 4 3 2 1

Contents

*To those on the spectrum and their families
who share freely, teach patiently, and
inspire us to think differently*

Acknowledgments

Many people helped us in the conceptualization and completion of this book, especially our friends and colleagues on the spectrum who teach us, challenge us, and help us to help others. In particular, we would like to acknowledge Jordan Ackerman, Jamie Burke, Michael John Carley, Judy Endow, Dena Gassner, Ruth Elaine Hane, Stephen Hinkle, Eugene Marcus, Barbara Moran, Jerry Newport, Sue Rubin, Jenn Seybert, Stephen Shore, and Liane Holliday Willey.

In addition, our spouses and children supported our work on this project by allowing us to write, proofread, edit, and chat on the phone even when it meant cutting into time that belongs to them. Thank you, Todd, Erma, Willa, Janet, Emma, Evan, and Brendan.

About the Authors

Dr. Paula Kluth is a consultant, advocate, researcher, and best-selling author whose specialties include differentiated instruction and supporting students with autism and those with significant disabilities in inclusive classrooms. A former university professor, Kluth now serves as an independent consultant working with educators, advocacy groups, and the families of students with disabilities.

Kluth is the author or coauthor of numerous books, including *"You're Going to Love This Kid!" Teaching Students with Autism in the Inclusive Classroom* (Brookes, 2003); *"Just Give Him the Whale!" 20 Ways to Use Fascinations, Areas of Expertise, and Strengths to Support Students with Autism* (coauthored with Patrick Schwarz; Brookes, 2008); *Joyful Learning: Active and Collaborative Learning in the Inclusive Classroom* (coauthored with Alice Udvari-Solner; Corwin, 2007), and *"A Land We Can Share": Teaching Literacy to Students with Autism* (coauthored with Kelly Chandler-Olcott; Brookes, 2007).

To contact Kluth for consulting or speaking engagements, please go to www.paulakluth.com.

John Shouse is parent to three children, including Evan, a thirteen-year-old son with autism. Shouse became involved in advocacy soon after Evan's diagnosis at age two. Shouse served as president of the Autism Society of Middle Tennessee for six years and for four years as a vice chair of the national board of the Autism Society of America. A 2003 graduate of Partners in Policymaking Leadership Institute, Shouse has been a passionate advocate for inclusive educational practices in local school districts across Tennessee and nationally. He is a frequent speaker at national and regional conferences on the special issues faced by fathers of children with autism and other disabilities and also on the joys and challenges of grandparenting a child with disabilities.

Introduction

With so much to know about autism, Aspeger syndrome, and life "on the spectrum," it is hard for those with autism labels, their families, and their teachers to know where to begin in a search for answers. In the past, it was difficult to find information anywhere. In the last few decades, there has been an onslaught of information, but not all of it has been as useful or as sensitive as we think it should be.

For this reason, we sat down to write a book that could give people quick answers and basic information in a way that is not only helpful but also thoughtful, informed, respectful, and accessible. We drew heavily from the words and experiences of people on the spectrum in order to create our recommendations and suggestions. We also looked at relevant research and kept our own lived experiences in mind. We think the result is a straightforward guide that will give readers a place to start when seeking answers about diagnosis, health and safety, life in the community and the home, teaching and learning, schooling, and relationships.

The first section of *The Autism Checklist* is about the label and diagnosis itself and contains information on characteristics, diagnostic tools, and related conditions. Two other sections of the book are designed to meet the needs of different populations. One section is devoted entirely to the needs of school personnel and will help teachers, paraprofessionals, therapists, social workers, psychologists, and administrators meet the unique needs of the student on the spectrum. More than anything else, we wrote the lists in this section with the aim of inspiring educators to create more relevant and gentle supports for students on the spectrum as well as more responsive classrooms. Another section was created for people on the spectrum and their parents. Our wish for this section was to provide suggestions that families can use to create experiences that are more safe, peaceful, and enjoyable. In this section, we cover everything from making the home comfortable to preparing for travel to advocating for your school-age child. Following these two sections, the reader will find a collection of lists offering "More Helpful Strategies for Home and School." The lists in this section relate to topics including, but not limited to, sensory issues, movement differences, communication, and helping individuals deal with stress and change. Because we know this book is likely to be a first-stop resource for our readers, the entire final section of the book is devoted to our recommendations for further study and exploration.

No matter your experience with or knowledge of autism, we believe you will find some tip, morsel of information, or resource in this book that answers a question, affirms a belief, or provides new insight. Moreover, we hope we can help you learn about and understand not only autism but the *individual* on the spectrum who is in your life.

The Autism Checklist

1

BASIC INFORMATION ON AUTISM AND ASPERGER SYNDROME

Introduction

1.1. What We Know About Autism

1.2. What Do We Mean by *the Autism Spectrum?*

1.3. Conditions Commonly Associated with Autism

1.4. Positive Traits Associated with Autism

1.5. Early Indicators of Autism

1.6. Autism Myths Versus Autism Facts

1.7. Tools Used in Autism Screening and Diagnosis

1.8. Social Differences

1.9. Communication Differences

1.10. Movement Differences

1.11. Sensory Differences and Sensitivity

1.12. Passions, Interests, and Rituals

Introduction

Autism is a fairly new diagnosis and has only been identified and studied since the 1940s. In every subsequent year more has been learned about autism and the autism spectrum, but most of what we know today has been learned in the last few decades. Families who had children in the 1950s, 1960s, and 1970s thus had a *very* different experience with diagnosis, treatment, and education than most families have today.

The past ten years in particular have seen an explosion of newspaper and magazine articles, books (including autobiographies), television programs, movies, and research studies on autism and Asperger syndrome. We know more than ever before, but at the same time this label and the disability are so new that our ignorance still surpasses our knowledge.

Adding to the difficulty of defining autism is considerable disagreement in the field about terminology, labeling, and the nature of life on the spectrum. Some camps, for instance, see autism as a disability, disorder, and collection of deficits. Others see it as a collection of differences, some valuable and useful, and others challenging. Even people on the spectrum may disagree about these conceptualizations, with some desiring a cure and others feeling pride in their diagnosis and valuing their autistic characteristics. And some have mixed feelings on the topic, feeling frustrated by symptoms of autism but grateful for the gifts it brings. We feel strongly that individuals on the spectrum, those who love them, those who support them, and those who engage in research on autism and Asperger syndrome must be aware of this diversity and not presume that any one of these perspectives is shared by everyone in the community. It should also be noted that not everyone on the spectrum experiences autism in the same way, so it is not only our worldviews but actual manifestations of autism that vary.

These particular differences made writing Section One particularly difficult, even from the starting point of deciding what language to use in our definitions and descriptions of the autism spectrum. We have handled this problem in many different ways. First of all, we use several different labels in this section in an attempt to illustrate the different ways people are seen and described in the literature. We sometimes talk about the *autism spectrum* and other times use *autism and Asperger syndrome*. The word *disorder*, however, is not used in this book at all, because we feel strongly that it is too limiting and, for some, it is clear a misnomer.

Another choice we have made in an attempt to honor the various ways our audience may see or understand autism is to keep our language fairly neutral (for example, using *differences* instead of *deficits*). We also feel this language is more precise, because those on the spectrum often have as many curious and unique abilities as they do struggles in the areas often seen as deficit areas. We have also tried to be fairly tentative when discussing what we know about autism, because it is constantly changing. Finally, as a researcher (Paula) and a parent of a child with autism (John), we tried to bring at least two different vantage points to the construction of these lists. To get a third and absolutely key perspective—the views of people on the spectrum themselves—we relied on observations from our own lives, conversations with friends and colleagues on the spectrum, and dozens of autobiographical works by people with autism and Asperger syndrome.

We hope the twelve lists included in Section One will clear up some of the confusion you may have about autism, Asperger syndrome, and related diagnoses. Because the autism spectrum is very complex and diverse, we have included several lists that are designed to simply provide information on the fundamentals of the autism spectrum, as in What We Know About Autism and What Do We Mean by *the Autism Spectrum*? One features conditions associated with autism, and a fourth contains all the positive traits associated with life on the spectrum. The final list that offers readers basic information is called Autism Myths Versus

Autism Facts and deals with misinformation about many aspects of autism including cognitive abilities, savant-type behavior and skills, and social tendencies.

Two lists in this section are reserved specifically for information on diagnosis and screening. One is dedicated to the early signs of autism and covers four different areas: language and communication, social skills, sensory issues, and behavior. The other features a range of tools used in screenings and in comprehensive evaluations.

The rest of the lists provide information on the various markers of autism, including communication differences; social differences; movement differences; sensory differences; and passions, interests, and fascinations.

We hope this opening section provides some clarification, answers questions, and sets up readers to learn and understand from the rest of the book.

1.1. What We Know About Autism

In 1943, Leo Kanner published the first paper identifying what we know today as *autism*. Kanner observed children who did not fit the patterns of other known disabilities. He thus invented a new category, which he called "early infantile autism." Independent of Kanner, Hans Asperger was making the same discoveries at the same time, but the patients he identified all had speech; Asperger syndrome, therefore, was used to describe that population. Following are some of the basic principles we have learned since the 1940s about autism and Asperger syndrome:

- Some people, including many on the spectrum, do not see autism and Asperger syndrome as disabilities. Some, in fact, understand autism as a natural part of what it is to be human, and many celebrate the gifts that are part of life on the spectrum.

- In 2007, the Centers for Disease Control and Prevention released data indicating that about one in 150 eight-year-old children in the United States was on the autism spectrum.

- Autism is sometimes called a developmental disability because it develops before age three and causes delays or significant differences in a variety of areas throughout the person's life span.

- The cause or causes of autism are unknown.

- Genetic origins of autism are suggested by two things: studies of twins and an increased incidence among siblings. It is unknown, however, exactly what role genetics play and whether there is a genetic root for each case of autism.

- Autism is diagnosed using interviews, observational tools, and checklists. There are no biological markers for autism or Asperger syndrome. There are no blood tests, brain scans, or other medical assessments that can be used to diagnose autism.

- Autism is often diagnosed by age three and in some cases as early as eighteen months. Researchers are currently working on assessments that could lead to diagnosis at age one or before.

- Many on the spectrum are not diagosed at all in childhood; it is not unusual for people to be diagnosed in adulthood (sometimes because their child gets a diagnosis). This is especially true for those with Asperger syndrome.

- Many more autism spectrum labels were assigned in the 1990s and 2000s than in previous decades. Between 1994 and 2006, the number of school-age children classified as being on the spectrum increased from 22,664 to 211,610. (IDEA data, 2009)

- Currently there are no medications that can "cure" autism or the related symptoms. Some medications, however, are helpful in easing or relieving related symptoms. For example, fluoxetine (Prozac) and sertraline (Zoloft) are approved by the FDA for children age seven and older with obsessive-compulsive disorder.

- There are many stereotypes associated with autism and Asperger syndrome. For instance, people may believe that everyone on the spectrum resists human touch. Or that they *all* love music. We know now, of course, that those on the spectrum are individuals with their own needs, abilities, gifts, talents, and challenges. There is no one set of difficulties that those with autism and Asperger syndrome experience and no one set of supports that will help every person with an autism spectrum label.

1.2. What Do We Mean by *the Autism Spectrum?*

The term *autism spectrum* is used to describe conditions including autism, Asperger syndrome, pervasive developmental disorder/not otherwise specified (PDD/NOS), childhood disintegrative disorder, Rett syndrome, and fragile X syndrome. Because different individuals with autism have very different symptoms, characteristics, and abilities, but also some core commonalities, autism has been described as being part of a spectrum. Following are some basic features of the conditions most commonly included in the autism spectrum:

- People with autism tend to have differences—some subtle and some very significant—in at least two realms: social and communication. They are also characterized as having unique differences in behaviors related to movement, objects, and routines.

- Asperger syndrome is characterized by differences in social interaction and patterns of behavior, interests, and activities, but no general delay in language, cognitive development, or adaptive behavior.

- PDD/NOS is diagnosed when the criteria are not met for autism or Asperger syndrome, but the individual exhibits the same types of differences as individuals with those diagnoses (such as differences in social skills, differences in communication skills, or differences in behaviors related to movement, objects, and routines). These individuals may, for instance, have speech problems, engage in repetitive behaviors, or have auditory sensitivity.

- Rett syndrome is also housed under the spectrum because individuals with this share a lot of characteristics with people with autism and Asperger syndrome. It is a unique developmental disability that is recognized in infancy and seen almost always in girls. It is often misdiagnosed as autism. Those with Rett syndrome exhibit symptoms similar to those diagnosed with autism, including repetitive movements (such as wringing or clasping their hands), gaze avoidance, and toe walking. These individuals also have weakened muscle tone and motor problems.

- Childhood disintegrative disorder is another condition that can also be found under the autism umbrella. Those labeled with childhood disintegrative disorder develop typically until age three or four and then seem to lose social, communication, and other skills. Childhood disintegrative disorder is often confused with late-onset autism because both involve normal development followed by a loss of skills. The differences—according to the medical profession—between autism and childhood disintegrative disorder are that autism typically occurs at an earlier age, it is less rare, and the loss of skills appears less dramatic.

- Fragile X is sometimes mentioned as part of the autism spectrum because some, but not all, individuals with that disability also have autism. Symptoms include characteristic physical and behavioral features and delays in speech and language development. Fragile X can be passed on in a family by individuals who have no apparent signs of this genetic condition. Fragile X is more common in boys. Physical characteristics include wider and longer ears and, in boys, enlarged testicles. Like those with autism, individuals with fragile X syndrome may have sensory motor problems, anxiety, and learning differences and may engage in repetitive behaviors.

1.3. Conditions Commonly Associated with Autism

Because autism itself is so complex and people with autism labels experience such different problems and have such varied needs, it can be difficult to see, sense, or observe physical problems, psychiatric conditions, or even disease in people on the spectrum. A person who is nonverbal, for instance, may be depressed but not physically able to cry easily or show changes in facial expression. Therefore, it is critical that all stakeholders, including people with autism labels, be aware of some of the most common co-occurring conditions. Some of those on the list may need special attention or support, and others will need to be simply acknowledged and considered in the development of education or vocational plans, in any medical treatment, or in the crafting of potential supports.

Following are some of the conditions that co-occur most frequently with autism and Asperger syndrome:

- Anxiety disorders
- Bipolar disorder
- Bowel disease
- Depression
- Dyslexia and other learning disabilities
- Gastrointestinal disorders
- Obsessive-compulsive disorder
- Phobias
- Pica
- Seizures and epilepsy
- Sleep disorders
- Tourette syndrome
- Tuberous sclerosis

1.4. Positive Traits Associated with Autism

We believe there is far too much discussion in both research and in the popular media about the deficits and struggles related to autism and not enough conversation about what people with autism *can* do or—perhaps even more critical—what they can often do *better* than those who are not on the spectrum. This is not to say that we don't see or understand all the difficulties people on the spectrum face. We have all too often seen the pain and challenge of the many sensory, communication, and movement problems that can be part of life with an autism label. However, we feel that learning about the abilities, strengths, and skills that may accompany autism is key. From this knowledge, supports can be built, understanding can be strengthened, and success can be realized. For this reason, we have compiled the following list on some of the most common positive traits associated with life on the spectrum:

- Artistic ability
- Attention to detail
- Creativity
- Energy
- Exceptional skill in mathematics, music, or learning new languages
- Fastidiousness
- Good memory
- Honesty
- Individuality
- Integrity
- Keen observational skills
- Methodical habits
- Neatness

- Nonjudgmental attitude
- Out-of-the-box thinking
- Passion
- Perfectionism
- Quirky sense of humor
- Refreshing perspective
- Reliability
- Stick-to-itiveness
- Strong mechanical skills

Keep in mind, people on the spectrum are individuals and these characteristics, like others, are only seen and experienced in some people. Like everyone else, people with autism and Asperger's syndrome have their own *unique* set of gifts.

1.5. Early Indicators of Autism

Other lists in this section provide detailed information about the many differences seen in and experienced by those on the spectrum. This particular list is not an attempt to illustrate all the characteristics seen in people with autism and Asperger syndrome; rather, it is a collection of things that parents and professionals often note in small children who are diagnosed. The following brief list can thus be used as starting point for considering an evaluation:

Language and Communication

- Starts talking later than other children or does not speak at all
- Does not respond to his or her name
- Does not babble, point, or make gestures that can easily be interpreted as communication
- Speaks with an unusual tone or rhythm (such as a singsong voice)
- Uses language in unique ways (such as "playing with" words, but not using them in a way that appears functional or communicating using lines from movies or even whole scripts)
- Appears to use his own language or method of communication (one that others don't understand or that only some people understand)
- Acquires language skills and then seems to lose them, either gradually or abruptly

Social Skills

- Is very independent
- Avoids eye contact and/or uses peripheral vision
- Connects with people in unique and very personal ways, such as pacing near them (instead of sitting next to them),

giving them objects (instead of hugging them), or playing a favorite game near others (instead of engaging in an activity or game with others)

- Plays with toys differently from most children (such as lining up toy cars or trucks instead of "driving" them on the floor or spinning a Frisbee instead of tossing it)
- Stays on task and focuses for long periods of time on certain activities (such as lining up marbles or filling up cups with water)
- Spends a lot of time and energy on organizing toys or environments
- Has a particular attachment to certain toys, objects, or events (such as examining a certain pamphlet repeatedly or carrying a favorite hairbrush around)
- Acquires certain social skills and then seems to lose them, either gradually or abruptly

Sensory Issues

- Resists some types of cuddling and holding and craves others (such as loving to be held tight and "smushed," but disliking holding hands)
- Enjoys feeling or rubbing certain textures, running hands through water, or pushing hands through sand
- Is unusually sensitive to light, sound, touch, and smell and may experience discomfort or even feel pain when experiencing "sensory overload"
- Resists certain foods and prefers a very limited diet
- Has a high tolerance for pain

Behavior

- Needs a lot of movement and exercise
- Toe-walks or moves in unusual ways

- Has sleep problems
- Engages in repetitive movements, such as rocking, spinning, or hand flapping
- Has specific rituals and routines (such as keeping all the doors in the house closed or organizing LEGOs by color)
- Appears frustrated or even distressed by changes in routines or rituals
- Fascinated by parts of an object, such as the spokes of a wheel or the moving pieces of a toy train bridge

1.6. Autism Myths Versus Autism Facts

More than ever before, information on autism is available to those seeking it. Sources for this information include the Internet, television, movies, books, and conferences. With this avalanche of research, how-tos, and stories, however, come not only accurate answers but misinformation as well. In the following list, we do our best to clear up some of the most common myths about autism.

Myth: Most individuals with autism have the same characteristics, needs, and strengths.

Fact: Because those on the spectrum share so many traits, some may believe that "If you know one person with autism, you know them all." In other words, some may assume that if you meet one child on the spectrum, you will know what to expect when you meet another. Nothing could be further from the truth. If you know one person with autism, you know just one person with autism. Those on the spectrum are incredibly diverse in their abilities, gifts, struggles, and difficulties. This diversity is one of the reasons diagnosis is so complicated; some on the spectrum find snuggling and hugging pleasant, others find it overwhelming. Some individuals are very precision-oriented and desire order in all areas of their lives; others are more flexible and seemingly unbothered by clutter or disorganization. In sum, people with autism are an incredibly diverse population.

Myth: Students with autism are often "in their own world" and become easily detached from people and experiences in their environment.

Fact: It is certainly true that people with autism report "slipping away" and focusing inward at times (especially in response to stress, boredom, or frustration). It is also true, however, that those who seem to be inattentive or focused elsewhere are sometimes simply unable to attend visually or maintain body language that others associate with focus, attention, interest, and engagement. Gaze avoidance, for example, can mean simply that the person cannot listen to the speaker and process her message while taking in all of the nonverbal communication in the eyes and face. So in order to listen to the verbal communication, the individual may look away. Similarly, a child who is flipping his fingers in front of his eyes and has his back turned toward the teacher may be very much aware of and tuned into the lesson. In fact, in some cases and for some people these behaviors may reflect the child's attempt to stay seated and calm. The repetitive behavior may in fact help the person relax and listen longer than if she were sitting still or facing the teacher.

For others, this detachment can be a form of protection. A child may focus inwardly because of loud noises in the environment or because of an inability to comprehend a novel situation. In these instances, blocking out external stimuli could be viewed as a helpful competency or skill and should therefore not necessarily be seen as evidence that the person does not want to socialize, be with others, or engage with the group.

Myth: Those on the spectrum prefer to be isolated and are not interested in socializing or having friends.

Fact: Children and adults on the autism spectrum often have a strong desire for friendship and socialization, but struggle to learn or use the behaviors needed to cultivate relationships or "operate" in a social situation. As John Elder Robison, a man with Asperger syndrome, notes in his autobiography, "I can't speak for other kids, but I'd like to be very clear about my own feelings. *I did not ever want to be alone.* And all those child psychologists who said, "John prefers to play by himself" were dead wrong. I played by myself because I was a failure at playing with others" (Robison, 2007, p. 211). What many on the spectrum need, therefore, is help with developing social skills and with interpreting social behavior. Those of us without autism labels may also need to open our eyes to the fact that each individual socializes differently. Not everyone likes to socialize by attending parties or engaging in long conversations. Many would rather connect by playing a game, taking a quiet walk, or simply by listening to music with others.

Myth: Most adults on the spectrum do not have a high quality of life.

Fact: Many people on the spectrum lead full and satisfying lives. More than ever before, people on the spectrum are pursuing postsecondary education, are employed in fields that interest them, and are living outside their family home independently or with support. Those on the spectrum are also enjoying a more robust social life than would have been possible in years past. Many marry and have children as well. People with autism have been successful across different professions and are particularly well represented in the computer industry in academia, in engineering, and in the sciences. It should also be noted that some of the leading minds in the field of autism are on the spectrum as well.

Along with this good news, it is also true that many people on the spectrum continue to face barriers to an appropriate education, a satisfying community life, and employment. Not only do many people on the spectrum need access to more options for supports and services in their lives, but there is also much work to be done in the way of advocacy. Negative stereotypes and misconceptions of autism often lead to missed opportunities, exclusions, and even abuse. So, while quality of life has improved for many, the journey to a full life continues for others.

Myth: All people on the spectrum are savants with amazing talents and gifts.

Fact: Most people with autism do not possess the extraordinary talents that are so often associated with life on the spectrum.

Most people, that is, are not able to play musical instruments without instruction or solve complicated equations without putting pencil to paper. An awful lot of people on the spectrum, however, are very skilled, capable, and gifted in areas that their peers outside the spectrum are not. For instance, many have exceptionally sensitive hearing or notice details that others miss, some are very good at keeping things organized, and others have a razor-sharp memory.

Myth: Many children and adults on the autism spectrum have cognitive disabilities or "mental retardation."

Fact: The truth is that we need to learn a great deal more than we currently know. For many individuals on the spectrum, especially those without reliable communication, there is no test that can measure what they know and can do. Therefore, most of the instruments used in evaluations measure autism *symptoms* as much as, if not more than, *abilities*. On top of the inadequacy of the instruments used in these assessments, many aspects of the evaluation process itself make accurate assessment challenging, if not impossible. There are many barriers to accurate testing for students with autism, including problems with language (such as understanding directions). In addition, many children and adults with autism cannot participate in many assessments due to movement problems, sensory differences, or related difficulties. It is not uncommon for a student with significant disabilities to get a low score on an instrument because she did not have a reliable pointing response, but was able to point. In other words, when asked to point to a monkey, some students point to a giraffe instead, even though they know which image is the monkey. This type of problem with motor planning is widely reported by people with autism.

1.7. Tools Used in Autism Screening and Diagnosis

No specific medical tests are available to diagnose those on the autism spectrum, so these labels are assigned based on the observations of parents, physicians, and others, along with assessments of developmental progress. The two steps to diagnosis are screening and comprehensive evaluation.

Screening

In most cases initial screening will be done by a family physician. In recent years tools have been developed to better identify children not just with autism but with Asperger syndrome as well. Screening instruments do not provide a diagnosis but help parents, physicians, and others determine whether the individual needs a comprehensive diagnostic evaluation. It is important to remember that many of the screening instruments cannot identify all children on the spectrum, especially those with Asperger syndrome. Following are just a few of the many available screening tools:

- Ages and Stages Questionnaires® (ASQ-3™)

  ASQ is a tool for screening infants and young children for developmental delays during the first five years of life. This test focuses on communication, gross and fine motor skills, social skills, and problem solving. This questionnaire can be purchased at www.agesandstages.com

- Australian Scale for Asperger's Syndrome (ASAS)

  This twenty-five-item questionnaire is designed to identify behaviors and abilities indicative of Asperger syndrome in school children ages six through twelve. It takes five to ten minutes to complete and is available at www.udel.edu/bkirby/asperger/aspergerscaleAttwood. html

- Autism Behavior Checklist of the Autism Screening Instrument for Educational Planning (ABC-ASIEP-3)

    The ABC consists of several behavior descriptions in five areas and is used to conduct a structured interview with a parent or other caregiver. It is less effective with high-functioning forms of autism. Available at www.proedinc.com

- Childhood Asperger Syndrome Test (CAST)

    These thirty-nine questions, designed for parents to answer about their children (ages four through eleven), are related to the core features of the autism spectrum. If parents suspect autism, they can complete this test and take it to their family doctor or pediatrician. It is available at www.autismresearchcentre.com/tests/cast_test.asp

- Checklist of Autism in Toddlers (CHAT)

    The CHAT is a screening tool developed for pediatricians to use at the eighteen-month checkup for children. Clinicians complete five items based on observation and ask parents to answer yes or no to an additional nine items. It is available for free at www.depts.washington.edu/dataproj/chat.html

- Modified Checklist for Autism in Toddlers (M-CHAT)

    A revised CHAT with additional questions is now available that may pick up more cases of autism and Asperger syndrome. It is available free at www.firstsigns.org/downloads/m-chat.PDF

- Parents' Evaluation of Developmental Status (PEDS)

    The Parents' Evaluation of Developmental Status is designed to assist parents determine whether their child has developmental delays. The questionnaire contains only ten questions and can be used for children from birth to eight years of age. The PEDS takes only about two minutes to administer and score if conducted as an interview. More information about PEDS can be found at www.pedstest.com.

- Social Communication Questionnaire (SCQ)

  The Social Communication Questionnaire, formerly known as the Autism Screening Questionnaire, contains forty items that are useful in identifying possible pervasive developmental disorders. This forty-item yes-or-no questionnaire is focused on communication and social skills and can be completed by a parent or primary caregiver in less than ten minutes. The SCQ determines whether a child or adolescent should be referred for a complete diagnostic evaluation. Get the SCQ at www.wpspublish.com

Comprehensive Diagnostic Evaluation

A comprehensive evaluation includes observations by your pediatrician and interviews with you as parents to find out more about your child's developmental history. It should also include assessment of language and speech and the use of one or more autism diagnostic tools. The second stage of diagnosis must be comprehensive in order to accurately rule in or rule out an autism spectrum condition or other developmental difference. This evaluation may be done by a multidisciplinary team that includes a psychologist, a neurologist, a psychiatrist, a speech therapist, or other professionals who diagnose children on the spectrum.

- Autism Diagnostic Observation Schedule (ADOS)

  ADOS is a standardized instrument for diagnosis of autism. It is used with children older than age two. General ratings are provided for four areas: reciprocal social interaction, communication and language, stereotyped or restricted behaviors, and mood and nonspecific abnormal behaviors. ADOS measures both nonverbal and preverbal communication components and should be conducted by clinicians who have been intensively trained to assess the child's use of language. Get more information about the ADOS at www.wpspublish.com

- Autism Diagnostic Interview–Revised (ADI-R)

    The ADI-R has been used by clinicians for decades and is used for the purposes of formal diagnosis. The ADI-R consists of ninety-three questions that fall under one of three functional domains: language and communications; reciprocal social interactions; and restricted, repetitive, and stereotyped behaviors and interests. The ADI-R can be purchased at www.wpspublish.com

- Childhood Autism Rating Scale (CARS)

    Developed over a fifteen-year period using more than 1,500 cases, CARS includes items drawn from five prominent systems for diagnosing autism. The CARS targets the child's body movements, adaptation to change, listening response, verbal communication, and relationship to people. This fifteen-item behavior rating scale helps to identify children older than age two with autism and to distinguish them from other children with disabilities who do not have autism. The CARS is available at www.wpspublish.com

- Gilliam Autism Rating Scale (GARS)

    The GARS helps to identify and diagnose autism in individuals ages three through twenty-two. The entire scale can be completed and scored in five to ten minutes. The instrument consists of forty-two items describing the characteristic behaviors of persons with autism. The items are grouped into three subscales: stereotyped behaviors, communication, and social interaction. Learn more about the GARS at www.pearsonassessments.com/gars2.aspx

1.8. Social Differences

It is often reported that students with autism are not interested in social relationships. Although some individuals with autism do report that they need time alone or that some social situations are challenging, many of these same individuals also state that they crave social interaction and friendship. Thus, it is possible for a person with autism to both struggle with and want relationships. This tension in personal life is one of many that may be experienced by a person on the spectrum. Following are some other common social differences experienced by people on the autism spectrum:

- Some may find social situations difficult because they lack the skills necessary for successful typical social interactions. A person may be unable to successfully read social overtures, participate in the give and take of conversation, or understand how to make small talk.

- Conversations in general can be overwhelming for people on the spectrum. Some people have a difficult time figuring out whether and when others are inviting them to participate in an exchange or knowing whether and how to enter or exit the conversation.

- Some of the norms of social behavior may also be hard for a person with autism to learn, manage, or use. For instance, a child may love to be with her classmates and really want to go to Friday night football games, but struggle so much with learning the rituals of cheering and fandom and figuring out the rules of small talk and "football speak" that she finds the evenings stressful and unpleasant. In some cases, people on the spectrum may find these behaviors too challenging to learn, and others may find that they are not comfortable engaging in them once they are learned, so they will resist using them. For instance, many on the spectrum find eye contact very uncomfortable. These individuals may find that they can attend better to the speaker when they are looking away from the person's face. This accommodation can be very helpful to the person with autism, but it can be misunderstood if the conversation partner doesn't know about it.

- Individuals with autism may struggle to read subtle social signals or to decode what they experience as social secrets. For instance, if a conversation partner yawns or begins putting on a jacket, most people would read this as a signal that the partner is getting ready to end the conversation and go home. For some individuals with autism, such subtle signs are hard to read, so they may not bring the conversation to a close (even when the other person adds, "Well, I'd better go").

- Students with autism may also struggle socially because those around them don't understand their attempts to be social or to interact. Some children, for instance, like to socialize with their father by playing a game or tossing a ball around. A child with autism might do the same *or* might try to show the same connection, affection, and desire for togetherness by following dad around the house, walking circles around him, watching him do projects, or bringing him a favorite object or toy.

- Play may look very different among those on the spectrum. Individuals with autism and Asperger syndrome may not play symbolically as other children do, for instance—that is, the child with autism may not feed the baby doll or pretend to grill a hamburger on the play stovetop. This does not mean, however, that they are not creative or imaginative in their play. Some show their creativity in the things they build or in the unusual ways they engage with their materials. A child may make a tower out of train tracks, for instance.

- Some sources suggest that those on the spectrum lack empathy or are egocentric. Although we know that some on the spectrum report struggling to see the viewpoint of another person, we also feel that the issue of empathy is sometimes overstated or misrepresented. While some on the spectrum are certainly more inwardly focused, some of the reported problems with empathy could also be seen as problems of expression. In other words, those with autism might have problems understanding empathy and feeling it, and just as many might simply have problems *showing* concern and care. In other words, a child might know that his sister is sick and care about her person and her suffering, but not know how to offer comfort (or even be aware that he should). Our loved ones and friends on the spectrum are some of the most empathetic and caring people we know and, in some cases, we have met many people who claim they are so attuned to the feelings of others that they themselves can feel emotional distress just by being around others who feel this way.

For recommendations on how to support or help someone in the area of social skills, see Checklist 4.7: Strategies for Encouraging and Supporting Social Relationships and Checklist 4.8: Strategies for Building Social Skills, both in Section Four.

1.9. Communication Differences

Individuals on the spectrum may have unique challenges with both verbal and nonverbal communication (such as facial expressions and body language). Some problems with verbal communication include difficulties with word retrieval, fluency, and speaking in general. Some of the problems with nonverbal communication include using gestures and making eye contact. Following are the communication differences most frequently experienced by people on the autism spectrum:

- Commonly, the tone of voice of a person with autism fails to accurately reflect her feelings. This can be problematic for a variety of reasons. Those on the spectrum may be seen as cold, aloof, uncaring, or unfeeling, simply because they cannot easily modulate their voice. They may also be seen as odd (and even intellectually disabled) because of the quality of their voice, especially if they use a monotone, singsong, flat, husky, or very unusual-sounding voice. Poor control of volume or intonation is also common.

- Some on the spectrum have difficulty modulating facial expression. Similar to problems with voice modulation, having little or no control over facial expression can be devastating because communication partners may believe the person with autism does not feel. In other words, the inability to express emotion is often assumed to be a lack of experiencing emotion. Again, many with autism report sadness and frustration about living with this movement problem.

- Some children (especially those with Asperger syndrome) speak like "little professors" or little adults. They may use sophisticated vocabulary, have clear and precise prounounciation, and be able to carry on a long and impressive conversation about a range of topics and especially about their topics of interest.

- Some people have trouble processing speech at times. An individual may not respond to his own name or may hand you a fork when you ask for a spoon. In most cases, people who behave in these ways are not experiencing hearing problems—they are experiencing processing difficulties. They have a hard time making sense of some of the sounds, words, or sentences they hear. Or they may understand what they are hearing, but are not able to respond appropriately. In other words, a person who knows that you are asking her to shut the door may unintentionally shut the window instead. Donna Williams, a woman on the spectrum, calls these "misfires" and admits that she has experienced them regularly: "I've said things like 'I want my shoes' when I meant 'I want my jacket' and been surprised to get things I apparently asked for" (Williams, 1996, p. 89). Because of these problems, individuals on the spectrum may seem inattentive or stubborn at times.

- Students with autism also have difficulty understanding some types of language. For instance, students with autism interpret language quite literally, so they may need help understanding figurative language and idioms (such as "sitting on the fence" or "hold your horses"), metaphors (such as "he was on fire"), jokes or riddles, phrases or slang expressions with double meanings, and sarcasm (as when we say "How graceful!" to someone who has just tripped).

- Some students repeat phrases or expressions over and over again across weeks, months, and even years as when the teacher says, "Be a gentleman" to the student, and he repeats this every time his manners are corrected for the next several years. Others repeat words, phrases, or expressions immediately after hearing them. For example, when the pastor says, "Good morning, everyone," and the individual with autism repeats, "Good morning, everyone." This phenomenon is called echolalia. If the student uses the words or phrases immediately after hearing them, the behavior is considered immediate echolalia. When the student repeats something that was said hours, days, weeks, or years ago, it is called delayed echolalia.

- Students who struggle with speech are sometimes blamed for saying inappropriate things or for not trying hard enough to speak "the right way." Some people who use language in unusual ways may even be assumed to be mentally retarded. For instance, a teacher who hears a student repeat "Oh, go fly a kite" several times might assume the student is not smart enough to know that his speech is silly or inappropriate. People with autism, however, often report that they have little or no control over their speech or that they have to use the speech they have because they lack specific words or phrases (the person cannot say, "I want to go to the park," for example, but he can say, "go fly a kite").

For recommendations on how to support or help someone improve communication skills, see Checklist 4.5: Strategies for Encouraging and Facilitating Communication and Checklist 4.6: Strategies for Supporting Those Without Reliable Communication, both in Section Four.

1.10. Movement Differences

Movement differences encompass both excessive atypical movement and the loss of typical movement and involve difficulties with starting, stopping, combining, executing (speed, control, target, and rate), and switching. These difficulties with movement may impede postures, actions, speech, thoughts, perceptions, emotions, and memories (Donnellan & Leary, 1995; Leary & Hill, 1996). Following are the movement differences most frequently experienced by people on the autism spectrum:

- Individuals with movement differences experience a host of problems, including but not limited to walking with an uneven gait, engaging in excessive movements (such as rocking, hand flapping, or pacing), producing speech that is unintentional, stuttering, or struggling to transition from room to room or situation to situation.

- The complexity of movements that are disturbed can range from simple movements (such as raising one's hand) to movements affecting overall levels of activity and behavior (such as completing a task). Many individuals who experience movement disturbance also report differences in internal mental processes such as perception and changes in attention, consciousness, motivation, and emotion.

- Motor clumsiness is part of movement differences. Those on the spectrum may be delayed in acquiring motor skills that require motor dexterity, such as opening a jar or buttoning a shirt.

- People with autism may appear awkward or uncomfortable in their own skin. They may be poorly coordinated, have an odd or bouncy gait or posture, poor handwriting, or problems with visual-motor integration, visual-perceptual skills, and conceptual learning.

- Many with autism experience these movement problems constantly. Although all of us may struggle to combine thoughts and movements, engage in excessive pencil tapping or nail biting, get lost in repetitive or obsessive thoughts, or sing the same tune repeatedly without realizing it, we are seldom negatively affected by these experiences. Many people with disabilities do experience serious movement problems, however, and are affected by them significantly and chronically.

- Atypical movements often mask the competence of individuals who exhibit them and may have an impact on their ability to communicate and relate to others. For example, "delay in responding or inability to regulate movements may affect the ability to turn attention from one event to another in a timely fashion, or use conventional signs of communication" (Donnellan & Leary, 1995, p. 42). In many cases, these movement differences are assumed by observers to be symptoms of mental retardation (Donnellan & Leary, 1995) when they are in fact symptoms of autism.

- A person with movement problems may find it difficult to know where parts of his body are in space without looking at them. He might also find it difficult to attend to, label, and interpret the signals of his body and may not recognize particular messages as feelings indicating his mental state (such as fear or frustration) or sensations indicating the physical states of his body (such as pain).

- Repetitive behaviors are seen in individuals on the spectrum. Rocking, hand clapping, finger flicking, or arm flapping are examples. Some repetitive behaviors are signals of distress. They may also be signs that the individual is bored or disengaged. Repetitive behavior can also be a kind of pleasant escape. The person may enjoy the sensation or it may be a tool for relaxation. When repetitive behaviors are being used to manage stress, they should be seen as purposeful and not as things to "extinguish."

- Crying or screaming that seems inappropriate or unprompted often occurs among those with movement problems. Some of this may be a result of discomfort, anxiety, pain, or confusion. In other instances, individuals may scream or even bang their heads in order to feel "organized" or to become more aware of and in control of their own bodies. As Birger Sellin, a man with autism, shares, "[I] am not hurting anyone when [I] scream and [I] need to do it so much to get my balance" (1995, p. 216).

- Inappropriate laughter is often seen in people with movement differences. This behavior appears to many observers to be evidence that the person is carefree or thinks others' behavior is funny. In reality, many on the spectrum indicate that unprompted laughter (especially under stressful circumstances) is actually a signal of distress, panic, or fear.

- Self-injurious behavior may be seen when the student is experiencing extreme anxiety or frustration.

For recommendations on how to support people with movement problems, see Checklist 4.9: Addressing Movement Differences in Section Four.

1.11. Sensory Differences and Sensitivity

People on the spectrum may have difficulties and sensitivity in one or more areas. Individuals may have visual or auditory sensitivity, difficulties with their olfactory system, or unusual responses to touch and temperature. Their sense of taste and thus their eating habits may also be affected. Following are the primary sensory differences experienced by people on the autism spectrum:

- Certain kinds of touch may be very difficult for people on the spectrum. Firm touch may be preferred over gentle touch, for instance. Unexpected touch can also be a challenge for some.

- Some people on the spectrum find the feel of certain clothes unbearable. People with autism may want to wear the same clothes over and over again, may prefer very soft garments, and may enjoy the sensation of certain fabrics over others.

- Some clothing may also be very soothing to a person with autism. The cling or grip of Lycra (such as bike shorts) can feel soothing to a person with sensory problems.

- Tactile problems may be apparent when the individual with autism avoids or prefers certain foods. The texture of food is very important to some and may even result in some individuals eating a very limited diet (only noodles and oranges, for instance).

- The sense of taste is often affected in people with autism. Differences in this area are often apparent in how the person prepares food. Some enjoy their food as bland as possible, while others use amounts of spices and seasonings that would be intolerable for many people.

- Temperatures can have a strong effect on people with autism. Some cannot tolerate, for instance, sitting too close to air conditioners or heaters. Cool or warm blasts, for some, can feel downright painful. It is important to realize, however, that the same sensation can feel very pleasant to another person on the spectrum.

- A range of noises and sounds may cause anxiety in a person on the spectrum with autism, including sounds that seem benign and even unnoticeable to the average person. For instance, a person might be completely distressed by the sound of a pencil moving across a tablet. And sounds we all may find annoying or painful such as a siren, alarm, or chalk screeching on the chalkboard can send the person with autism into an absolute panic. Sounds that tend to bother a lot of people on the spectrum include crying babies, vacuum cleaners, dishwashers, washing machines, lawnmowers, heavy equipment and sounds related to demolition and construction, alarms, sirens, repeating beeps (as made by large vehicles backing up), the buzz of fluorescent lights, and large or particularly noisy crowds.

- Vision may also be affected. Students may be sensitive to certain types of light, colors, or patterns. For instance, if a person is wearing an outfit with several bright colors or with big patterns, it may be hard for some on the spectrum to look at that person. Another vision-related issue some have concerns visual clutter. Some people become overwhelmed in disorganized or confusing spaces and crave order and neatness.

- Those with autism and Asperger syndrome may also have a heightened sense of smell. The individual may find some smells unbearable and others pleasant, helpful, or calming. Smells that may bother students include air fresheners, art products, perfumes or colognes, food, school supplies, cleaning agents, chemicals, pet odors, and plants or flowers.

- The pain threshold for a person with autism may be different from the thresholds of people without these labels. A person on the spectrum may gash herself or even break a bone, yet never cry out in pain. At the same time, a gentle hug or light tickle on the arm can make the same person jump, scream, or run away.

- When overloaded, people with autism may have trouble concentrating or may feel tired and irritable. Too much sensory overload may lead to behavior problems, emotional outbursts, or even physical pain.

For recommendations on how to support people with sensory differences, see Checklist 4.10: Addressing Sensory Issues: Visual; Checklist 4.11: Addressing Sensory Issues: Tactile; Checklist 4.12: Addressing Sensory Issues: Auditory; and Checklist 4.13: Addressing Sensory Issues: Olfactory; all in Section Four.

1.12. Passions, Interests, and Rituals

Many individuals with autism have deep interest in one or a variety of topics. Some interests are commonly seen across individuals with autism. Some of the most common of these are trains, weather, and animals. Other interests seem more unique to an individual person. One person we know loves to talk about and study John Wilkes Booth. Another is passionate about socket wrenches. Following are more of the passions, interests, and rituals enjoyed by people on the autism spectrum:

- Some of the most common fascinations across people with autism are trains, vehicles, transportation systems, machines, weather, natural disasters, geography, astronomy, gadgets, animals, nature, dinosaurs, computers, historical dates or events, calendars, timetables, numbers, chemistry, cartoon characters, drawing, artists, music, pop stars, and television shows (Hippler & Klicpera, 2004; Mercier, Mottron, & Belleville, 2000). Some people remain interested in one area for their entire lives; for others, interests change and evolve from month to month or year to year.

- Individuals may also have rituals that are important in their lives. Some people have rituals for organizing their time and the space around them; others have rituals around how and when they engage in certain behaviors. Individuals on the spectrum (and those without autism labels too) may have rituals attached to any number of activities in their lives, including eating (such as separating food by colors), numbers and counting (such as insisting on leaving the house exactly at 7:35AM), dressing (such as always putting socks on first), cleaning (such as vacuuming in the same pattern each time), exercising (such as walking the same number of laps each day), shopping (such as doing errands in a certain order), or interacting with others (such as preferring to talk to people with names that begin with B before talking to others).

- Other types of ritual you may see in students with autism involve repetitive behaviors. An individual may spend a lot of time engaged in certain tasks such as turning in circles, spinning a toy, playing in water or sand, stacking things up, or putting things in order.

- Individual objects may also be dear to the person on the spectrum. Some individuals carry around tokens, trinkets, or comfort items. We have known individuals on the spectrum who have carried wrenches, plastic money, tennis balls, wristbands, rubber bands, bracelets, marbles, paintbrushes, watches, rocks, video boxes, strings, and mechanical pencils, to name only a few. Sometimes the person is content to have special items on his person. Others may want to use the item to fidget and may like the sensation of holding or playing with their favorite things.

- Collections may be part of the life of a person with autism or Asperger syndrome. The individual may collect things that are commonly associated with hobbies such as dolls, coins, CDs, movies, photographs, or stamps. It is not uncommon, however, to meet a person with autism who has a very unique collection that would not be seen across many different individuals. For instance, people on the spectrum may collect pencil stubs, antique railroad lanterns, pieces of denim, magazines from 1999, or gum wrappers.

For recommendations on how to support the fascinations and special interests of individuals on the spectrum, see Checklist 3.6: Addressing Student Passions and Fascinations in the Classroom in Section Three.

2

CHECKLISTS FOR PARENTS

Introduction

Just as every individual with autism is different, every family is different and must work to find the balance and create the life that works for them. What *is* required is to approach the challenges of creating that family life with both flexibility and a definite plan. (A good sense of humor helps too!)

The lists in this section address something that sounds almost too obvious to have to say. When a child is diagnosed with autism, it changes the family's life. It will change in ways both predictable and unpredictable. It will change in some ways that become obvious as soon as the parents first hear the word *autism* uttered with regard to their child. Some changes occur immediately, and others may not become obvious for months or even years.

The relationship of the parents with one another may change. The relationship between parents and their other children may change, as may the relationship between the child on the autism spectrum and his or her siblings. Extended-family relationships with grandparents, aunts, uncles, and cousins may change. And as you work to implement strategies and activities to best support your child with autism, many of the things that have been familiar family routines may require change as well.

To help families cope with some of these transitions, we offer a list titled After Diagnosis that can provide some first steps to confused and overwhelmed parents. Another list will help parents share the news with others, and still another will give moms, dads, and other family members ideas for getting help and gathering resources. A fourth list will help parents hone their advocacy skills.

We realize it is well beyond the scope of this book, or any book, to attempt a comprehensive one-size-fits-all approach to creating a loving, natural, accepting, and supportive home environment and family experience. Indeed, no such universal approach exists. What we do offer in Section Three, however, is a starting point and guidelines for families to craft their own approach. For example, one list, What Those on the Spectrum Need at Home, will give parents inspiration for daily living. On a more practical note, we offer lists on modifying the home, on safety around the house and in the community, and on helping your son or daughter learn at home. Finally, we have included lists to help families adapt as they travel, venture out into the community, and socialize with loved ones and friends.

Above all, parents of newly diagnosed children should remember that although a certain level of unpredictability has now become part of their lives, their child is still the same unique, fascinating, and wonderful person that he or she was before the diagnosis. The good news is that *many* families who receive a diagnosis on the autism spectrum for their child find that despite the challenges that arise, they are able to forge a stronger family bond and experience joy and love in new ways, as they help their child on the spectrum find his or her greatest level of independence, unique gifts and abilities, and personal fulfillment.

2.1. After Diagnosis

Remember that your child has not changed. After diagnosis, families may feel confused, frustrated, and even distressed, depending on the needs and struggles of their child. They may be unsure of where to turn, who to turn to, and even how to conduct day-to-day activities. Perhaps the most important thing to keep in mind is that the child you have after diagnosis is the same child you had before the diagnosis. She has the same gifts, abilities, idiosyncrasies, needs, and challenges. Move forward with activities and plans and do not limit time with others, experiences, travel, or special events unless necessary. Following are some basic pieces of advice to keep in mind after your child is diagnosed:

- Put the brakes on. It is, of course, necessary to begin to assemble supports and tap into resources after your child has been assigned a label. However, you don't need to do all those things the same day you get the diagnosis. Slow down and take time to read the information you have been given.

- Stop and ask. As you learn about your child's diagnosis and gather information from professionals, be sure that you understand *everything* that is being shared with you. Be sure to ask questions or request clarification any time you don't understand what you are hearing or reading.

- Educate yourself in ways that feel right for you. Read about the autism spectrum (we recommend autobiographies as a great starting point for parents with a new diagnosis; see Section Five for recommendations); watch a documentary film (see Section Five for recommendations); talk to other parents who have children on the spectrum; talk to someone on the spectrum; go to a conference related to autism; or simply surf the Internet to find out more about your son or daughter's specific needs, potential services, and local and national resources.

- Shop for support. There are many approaches to supporting children with autism. Start exploring these options by talking to local professionals, other families, and your family physician. Most families will want to start with some basic supports such as in-home occupational therapy or speech and language therapy. Preschoolers and school-aged children may be offered therapies through the school system.

- Think about telling your child. Depending on the age of your son or daughter, you may want to share information about the diagnosis immediately. Many individuals on the spectrum report that knowing about their label has been very beneficial throughout their lives, not only as a way to explain things that happen or that they experience, but also as a way to understand their own lives and form an identity. Further, knowing about one's diagnosis can potentially bring insight, solace, comfort, relief, and even support. Those who know about their label can then become knowledgeable about it, and those who become knowledgeable about it can learn strategies for coping, ideas for personal growth and even tips for success. This goes for children with more significant disabilities, as well as for those with Asperger syndrome. If an individual does not have reliable communication, we do not know what he or she knows or can learn. Therefore, the "least dangerous assumption" (Donnellan, 1984) is that she *does* understand, and parents should feel free to give information about the label, diagnosis, and characteristics of autism if it seems age-appropriate and if it may potentially help their child cope, learn, or grow.

2.2. Sharing the News

Decide who, when, and what to tell about your child's diagnosis. You don't have to tell everyone at once, and you don't have to tell them all in the same way, but it will help you avoid questions, uncomfortable moments, and certain types of advice if you simply share the news. You may want to sit down and have a heart-to-heart with some family members and friends. For others, you might find a group e-mail or a family newsletter an appropriate place to give the information. Share in a way that makes you and your child feel the most comfortable. Grandparents, in particular, may find the news of a diagnosis particularly difficult. Many of them grew up in a time when society thought differently about disability, and the resources we have today were nonexistent or accessible only to some. They will likely be feeling the same confusion, frustration, and distress as the parents and will also very likely be concerned about what this means for their own children. Following are some specific ideas for sharing the news about your child's diagnosis:

- Help others learn. Uncle John might want to see research on autism, and Grandpa might want to read stories about families who have children on the spectrum. Older siblings may want to surf the Web to learn more. Remember that everyone learns differently, so be prepared to provide a range of resources and materials (see Section Five for our recommendations).

- If it seems appropriate, involve your child in sharing the news. If you have shared the diagnosis with your youngster and he is interested in learning more and getting involved in self-advocacy, you might encourage him to play a part in educating others. This approach may not be appropriate if the diagnosis has come while your child is very young, but in some cases it can be very liberating and educational to make it a family affair.

- Don't leave out the good news. Share information and stories about your child that reflect both his challenges and his strengths. It is very important that those closest to you see and understand what is difficult for your child (such as dealing with loud noises and reading social situations), but also that they understand all the things your child likes, loves, can do, enjoys, excels in, and knows.

- Plan activities that help family and friends see your child at his or her best. For instance, if trains are a special interest of your child, invite the whole group when you head to the railroad museum.

- Teach by example. Involve your family and friends—and your child—in activities that will help educate them. For example, take them to conferences you attend (the Autism Network International and the Autism National Committee are two groups that run very autistic-friendly conferences), bring them to your meetings, and give them your favorite books to read.

- Go ahead and tell—it just might help. If you are a self-advocate reading this book, you have a whole range of decisions to make about disclosure as well. If you are a teen, you may be nervous about telling new friends or potential employers. If you are an adult, you may be unsure of how (or whether) to tell your family, romantic partners, spouses, or even children. We know there are many considerations to explore, but in general we believe that disclosure brings more benefits than risks. One of our favorite books on this topic is *Ask and Tell: Self-Advocacy and Disclosure for People on the Autism Spectrum* (Shore, 2004). This is a must-read for teens and adults on the spectrum, because it is written by many wise self-advocates and chock full of helpful hints.

2.3. Help for Families

Only thirty short years ago, families had few ways to get information about the autism spectrum and connect with others in the community. Support groups and national organizations were just getting started, few books existed on the topic, and few experts were available to guide and support families. Today, things have changed, and families can look to many organizations, print resources, Web sites, and experts for help. This list will help you begin your search.

- Go national. Organizations such as the Autism Society of America offer materials and resources for families just getting a diagnosis.

- Talk to other families. Perhaps the most powerful and helpful support available to families of newly diagnosed children is other parents of children on the spectrum. So many families, despite very busy schedules, are formally or informally available to offer advice and guidance and to share their personal experience. You may meet other parents through local groups, by taking your child to therapy or through friends and family. If you want to formally connect with another family, many organizations offer some type of family-to-family or parent-to-parent program where you can be assigned a mentor parent or mentor family.

- Check local advocacy and support groups. All groups have different functions, so make sure the ones you target will meet your needs. If you are seeking support as parents of a young child, look for a group with other parents of newly diagnosed children. If you are looking for help on finding an inclusive preschool for your child, then a cross-disability advocacy group might serve your needs better. To get the most out of your local resources look at groups focused on autism as well as those focused on people with other disabilities such as Down syndrome, learning disabilities, for instance.

- If you live in an area without a lot
  of resources such as a rural community, you may be able to
  find the support you need online. Message boards, listserves,
  and Web sites provide support to many families and
  individuals on the spectrum every day. Some who connect
  using these formats become virtual pen pals in addition
  to participating in the larger electronic communities.

- Go straight to the experts. People on the spectrum are
  probably the best sources of information, guidance, and wisdom available to us all. Many adults on the spectrum consult
  with families on a variety of issues. No adult on the spectrum
  should be expected to serve in this role, of course, unless they
  have expressed an interest in doing so or have decided to
  make a career of this work. If you do know of such individuals,
  it is our experience that counselors, social workers,
  teachers, behavior consultants, and educational consultants
  on the spectrum offer a perspective not otherwise available.

- Start your own community. If your specific needs are not being
  met through existing groups, consider starting your own.

2.4. What Those on the Spectrum Need at Home

As previously mentioned, the child with a diagnosis of autism is the same wonderful, kid that you had before the diagnosis. It will be important for parents and siblings to learn to (or continue to) have the highest expectations for the child with autism, while also understanding the challenges the child faces. According to V. Mark Durand's (2008) research on families, the highest predictor of the success or failure of any particular intervention or support is parental attitude: children were most successful when parents kept a positive outlook. A child on the spectrum also needs:

- Opportunities to have fun. Learn to appreciate the things that make your child on the spectrum happy and, if possible, get involved in those things yourself. Does he or she like swimming? Horseback riding? Doing puzzles? Going on hikes? Watching trains? Going to monster movies? Just as you would do with any child, find out what those things are and work to create opportunities to participate and engage in those activities. Even if your child's interest is simply watching the sprinkler oscillate, take some time to share the experience with him or her. For some kids on the spectrum, these favorites change frequently, and for others the things they enjoy now may become lifelong interests.

- Appreciation of his uniqueness. Don't look for the autism in *everything* the child does. Read up on and learn about age-appropriate behaviors and the stages of development for typical kids. Realize that children on the autism spectrum will likely be going through those stages too. They may go through them at different ages, in a different sequence, or in unique ways, but try to remember that not every quirky behavior or frustrating occurrence is attributable to autism.

- Opportunities to take risks. Don't overcompensate and don't overprotect. Yes, this is your precious child, and she may have a somewhat higher degree of vulnerability being on the autism spectrum, but it is important to learn about the concept of "dignity of risk." Try to remember that everyone needs a chance to fail from time to time, so that they can learn appropriate skills to cope with those failures. When learning new skills, no one is invariably successful the first time or every time, and learning to deal appropriately in those times when we do *not* succeed is very important. Learning these kinds of lessons at home in a reasonably safe environment can pave the way for a more successful experience when your child takes newfound skills out into the world.

- Encouragement of independence–avoid learned helplessness. Because many people on the spectrum have difficulty mastering what others consider simple tasks, the natural temptation for parents and family members is to want to do things for them. Rather, to foster independence, you should aim to create a mindset where you as a parent see even trivial tasks as opportunities to learn new skills. For very young children these things may be as simple as brushing their own teeth, bathing or showering, shampooing and brushing hair, getting dressed, and the like. As they grow, they can start to learn to get their own drinks or snacks, do laundry, organize their toys, or clean their own room. Try to always keep in mind (even in the most trivial of situations) that one of your most important long-term goals for your child should be his greatest degree of independence.

- Time out to "just be." Pay special attention to your own state of mind. Parents of children with disabilities or medical needs often have more stressors in their lives than parents of typical children. You are a family who has a member with autism. You are not a family who has become the living embodiment of all things autistic. Though it may feel necessary sometimes, you are not required to live, walk, talk, and breathe autism every minute of every day. Trying to do so will not only be overwhelming but it won't leave room for much else! It's okay to designate an "autism-free" zone or one night of the week where therapies, running to seminars, and research on the Web all take a backseat.

- Strive for balance. Although it is certainly important to see that your child on the spectrum is meaningfully engaged a significant portion of the day, it is also true that she deserves and needs some alone time or downtime. Maybe it's a time when she can play in her room or watch a video by herself. Siblings deserve this same consideration, and so do parents. Create scheduled opportunities for family members to have those needs met. At the same time, create some opportunities for the whole family to be together, laugh, enjoy, and just have fun.

2.5. Modifying the Home

Certain life events—such as bringing a baby home from the hospital or taking in a sick relative—require modifications of the home. Having a child with autism may be one of those events for some families. Some changes will be temporary as you move through a stage with your child, and others may be longer lasting. Following are some minor and somewhat significant changes you may need to make at home for a child on the spectrum:

- Create a retreat. Find a space where your child can relax after school. This may be a corner of the basement or a nook in the bedroom. Provide comfortable seating, some favorite materials (such as basketball magazines, multiplication flashcards, or rainbow photographs), and sensory supports such as a cup of straws to chew on, a favorite lotion, arm weights, a favorite hoodie, and small fidget toys.

- Do the same for mom and dad. Create a place where can relax too, perhaps a corner of a room or your own bedroom. Keep your own favorite things there and your own sensory supports (such as favorite treats, candles, or comfy chair).

- Post a family schedule or calendar. Your child will not only want to have a sense of where she needs to be and when, but will also find comfort in knowing the comings and goings of all family members (especially mom and dad). It is far more traumatic for most kids on the spectrum to have mom leave for a week on business if they don't know in advance that it is happening, can't grasp how long it will go on, and are not emotionally prepared for the transition.

- Take a lesson from the teacher. No matter how old your child is, organize his bedroom like a kindergarten classroom. Bins and drawers should be clearly labeled (especially for young children), and there should be a place for everything. This level of organization will help him not only to find things independently, but also to take care of the space and materials more easily.

- Choose furniture carefully. Some children may use chairs or tables to climb to higher spaces in order to get favorite foods, toys, or materials or to see something that captures their interest. Others, for sensory reasons, may like the feeling of bouncing on the beds or getting squished in the cushions of sofas and chairs. For these reasons, if you are in the market for furniture, consider that less expensive furniture might be more suitable—at least in areas that are used often by children. At the very least, buy for durability as much as for appearance!

- Try using some music as a tool for transitions, relaxing, and for other purposes as well. Experiment with different types of music that the whole family will enjoy at different times and across activities (such as soothing music to signal bedtime and big band music before leaving to visit Great Grandma).

- If you redecorate, let your child have a say as you choose paint colors or simply pick soothing shades of tan or cream.

- In the child's room, consider how to create the most peaceful space possible. You might install carpet to reduce noise, add blackout curtains to eliminate early morning light, and experiment with a sound machine to soothe nerves and encourage uninterrupted sleep.

2.6. Safety at Home

Most parents of young children are familiar with the process of childproofing the home, and many products and informational resources are available to provide guidance in this regard. Parents of children on the autism spectrum should be aware that there may be an increased need to employ some of these standard measures for their children and to engage in these activities. They may also find they need to continue with these measures beyond the age when other children have outgrown the need for them. Following are the primary safety considerations at home for children on the spectrum:

- If you have a lot of knickknacks, glass, vases, or other decorative objects around, getting new, more durable decor. Instead of spending precious time and energy worrying about potential disasters, either put fragile things far out of reach or simply decorate with objects that can be handled, dropped, and spilled (such as small wooden figures, empty bowls, and stacks of books).

- Use visuals to teach boundaries and keep kids safe. Use dividers, colored tape, symbols, and signs to show areas and items that are off limits. For example, colored tape can be stuck on the floor in front of a room that should not be entered (such as a basement workshop). It can also be used to create outlines on carpets or even on the driveway or lawn to show where toys or children should stay. Stop signs or no entry signs can be hung on doors, drawers, cupboards, appliances, and even on power tools. Colored dots or stickers can be used in the same way. For instance, one family we know used colored dots to teach their small child which toys and toy bins were appropriate for him to access. His older sibling's items (particularly games with small parts) were coded with a different color.

- Some on the spectrum like to create or experiment with cutting or ripping materials. Individuals may like the sounds or the sensation of tearing or using a scissors. Be sure to provide a safety scissors and an array of acceptable materials for this activity, and be sure to supervise when the child is involved in these projects.

- Childproof everything electrical. This is important for all children, of course, but many kids with autism have great interest in and even expertise in electronics and may find playing with wires and sockets irresistible. You will also need to hide cords behind furniture and under rugs (or cover them with tubing) to make them less tempting. Finally, be sure that electronics are secure. If a stereo system, for instance, is stacked precariously on a table, the gadget lover in your family can be harmed while trying to unstack, explore, or untangle the components.

- Lock up the toxins. Even if your children are older, put locks on cabinets that contain medicines, cleaning products, and other potential poisons. Colorful bottles and interesting-looking tablets and capsules can be fascinating to many children, including those on the spectrum. Children and teens may be intrigued by the textures and tastes of these items and, for those who don't read, it can be easy to confuse certain candies with certain medicines or even favorite juices with red, purple, and orange liquid medicines.

- Secure windows and doors. If your child with autism is prone to running or leaving the home without your knowledge, it may be a good idea to use locks that he or she cannot easily manipulate. Likewise, windows can be equipped with a variety of locks as well, available at your local hardware store. (This decision must be tempered with the idea that the child should have knowledge of how to get out in the event of a fire or other emergency.) One family became aware of how important it was to secure their windows when they received a frantic call from a neighbor who happened to look out and see that their child had climbed out a window and was perched on the edge of a second-story roof.

- Take out the glass. If your child has broken glass in the past or you fear that he or she might do so, consider replacing window panes with Plexiglas or even safety glass that will not shatter. These alternatives may be expensive, but will bring great peace of mind.

- Play "keep away." Some individuals with autism have a condition called pica, which means that they like to eat or taste nonfood items such as dirt, paint chips, chalk, coffee grounds, cigarette butts, ice, glue, hair, toothpaste, soap, or paper. Although consumption of some of these items is harmless, pica is considered to be a serious disorder that can result in significant health problems such as choking or lead poisoning. Some individuals may crave these items (or ingredients found in these items); others may just want the sensory experience that comes from chewing on or eating them. For instance, a person may not like the flavor of soap, but may crave the sensation of chewing on or biting into a bar of soap. If your child has this problem, be sure to assess your environment and keep potentially dangerous items out of her reach. Cigarettes, for instance, should never be left in an ashtray if they are tempting to your child. Liquid soaps can replace bars if needed. And coffee grounds should be thrown directly into the trash (and maybe into another container first to dull the scent) after the coffee is brewed.

2.7. Safety in the Community

All parents worry about safety in the community, and this worry can be exacerbated when your child cannot communicate reliably, cannot easily protect himself if needed, and becomes easily agitated in unfamiliar situations. To minimize worries and maximize safety, consider the following ideas:

- Provide identification. When out on trips with a child with limited communication skills, you may want to have your child either wear or carry some form of ID with her name and your contact information. There are a number of different kinds of specialized ID bracelets or devices commercially available for this purpose, even some fairly high-tech ones with the ability to track your child if you become separated. Iron-on labels are another option. Alternatively, you may simply choose to make up a small business card–sized ID card that can be carried in a backpack or pocket. Some children can be taught to utilize this card if they become lost or confused. One family we know created such a card by writing cell phone numbers, hotel numbers, and such on a laminated luggage tag that they then attached unobtrusively to a belt loop for use on trips to parks, shopping centers, and theme parks. This type of aid could be useful for short errands and longer trips as well. It can be especially helpful on vacations and trips to crowded public places where you can easily be separated from your child.

- Implement safeguards for children who like to explore. When children on the spectrum become independently mobile, it is not uncommon for them to wander and start to explore their environment. A child outside and away from your supervision who is also unable to adequately communicate information about who she is and where she lives is extremely vulnerable. Introduce your son or daughter to neighbors within a short radius of your home. For children who wander and do not have reliable communication, you may even want to make up a safety card with a picture of your child, relevant information about autism and her unique needs ("she communicates using sign language," for example), and any special concerns you may have (such as how she reacts to strangers or whether she tends to climb a lot or run into streets). To make this process as respectful as possible, make sure you include information about your child's personality, interests (such as "she loves the Rolling Stones"), and favorites (such as "she knows everything about game shows"). This flyer should also include contact information for you, your family, and who others should contact if you are unavailable. This safeguard can go a long way toward averting or mitigating a number of different unfortunate situations.

- When a child does not understand what firefighters, police officers, and paramedics do or why they do it, their presence can cause fear, anxiety, or even terror, especially in an emergency or stressful situation. Consider ways that you might teach about these professions and related safety rules and appropriate behaviors in the event of emergency situations. Such teaching can involve the use of social narratives, visual schedules, signs, or books and videos about people in the community. Your child needs to understand that when he encounters a safety professional, it is likely a very serious situation that requires his cooperation. Your child should also be taught the consequences of unsafe behaviors.

- As a more personalized approach, consider contacting your local fire or police station to ask if you can bring your child by for a quick visit and introduction. If the authorities agree (most will be delighted to do this for you), create a social narrative with your child beforehand about the trip or read a book about what first responders do. Ask ahead of time whether it might be appropriate for your child to put on a firefighter's helmet or sit in the police car. The goal is to familiarize both your child and the firefighters with each other, so that in the event of an emergency there is already a level of comfort on both sides. Be sure to leave one of the same safety cards you prepared for your neighbors at the station.

- Just as children need to learn about first responders, first responders often need more information about autism. Some local chapters of the Autism Society of America or other advocacy groups may already have an active program to teach autism awareness to police, fire, emergency medical, and other first-responder agencies. If they do, find out what the program provides and if they have any special materials available. You might even consider volunteering. The Autism Society of America offers good resources for this sort of activity at www.autism-society.org, under Preparedness Tips for First Responders. If there is no formal training being done in your area, don't give up; order or print out copies of the brochures and take stacks of them to the local police precinct, fire department, or emergency room, and ask that they be placed in a break room or other place where they are likely to be seen and read.

2.8. Adaptations at Family Events

Spending the summer at Aunt Sara's cabin? Invited to a family reunion? Need to make it through another birthday party for one of your nieces? With a few adaptations, some of these events can be survived—and even enjoyed—by the whole family. Following are some ideas to make family events more comfortable for your child on the spectrum:

- Keep special photo albums of family reunions, vacations, and holidays. Let your child with autism review the albums often so she gets to know names, faces, and places and feels comfortable returning to the homes of various family members and friends.

- Have a plan for taking a break when you are at the event. Is there a basement with a TV? A backyard with a swing set? A nearby park, playground, or nature trail? If you are going to be visiting for more than a day or so, investigate ahead of time the availability of preferred activities such as swimming, shooting baskets, and such. Explain to the family that the break is a necessary interruption in your time with them to ensure a successful and stress-free visit for your child.

- Ask friends and relatives how kid-friendly their home is before you get there. Be sure breakables are stored, candles are snuffed out, and anything that invites climbing is hidden.

- Shoot some footage of your children engaging in behaviors that you want to see at the event. If you want them to say (or sign or point to) "thank you" after opening a birthday gift, practice acting it out at home and then film the "scene" and watch the movie several times.

- Check to see if noisemakers will be given out (as with birthdays or New Year's Eve), warn your child in advance if so—or better yet, ask that noisemakers be given to children on the way out of the party and not used during the event.

- If you can, give your child a special job to do. This will make the event less overwhelming, possibly give her something to look forward to, and help her meet and interact with people in a less random and chaotic way. A small child can help set the table, keep drinks stocked in coolers, make name cards, or take pictures. An older child can shoot video, help with cooking, entertain younger kids, or run some type of activity (such as an egg hunt or a croquet tournament).

- If your child is nonverbal, have him bring pictures of a recent special day or a scrapbook of favorite things. This will give friends and relatives something to use as a conversation starter and help your child communicate with others about his life without your needing to be there to narrate.

- Bring some food items that your child can eat and will eat, especially if he or she follows a special diet.

2.9. Adaptations for Errands and Outings

Running errands is part of family life, but if your child struggles with waiting or gets anxious traveling in the car for long periods of time, you may need supports to get to the dentist, pharmacy, or grocery store without tears or frustration. Following are some ideas to make errands and outings less problematic for your child on the spectrum:

- Avoid unnecessary trips. For some children and for some families, a trip to the grocery store can seem more trouble than it's worth. In other words, three days without milk starts to seem like a small price to pay to avoid a little drama. Look into online options for grocery ordering (which is becoming more widely available, even in smaller cities), shopping (select all your holiday gifts in one evening), driver license and city sticker renewal, library book reservation, movie selection and delivery, and postage printing and home package pickup.

- Stay in. You may also want to consider services now offered at home that previously required a trip into the community. Some photographers will do family portraits in the home, a few dry cleaners now pick up and drop off, and in some communities milk delivery is making a comeback.

- Keep it simple. For most families, a day or entire morning of errands is probably too much. Instead, restrict outings to one or two errands per trip.

- Prioritize. If you do have two or three errands to run, do the most important one first. If you would love to get to the mall, but really need to get to the travel agent, go to the travel agent first and assess afterwards to see whether the crew is up for a shopping trip.

- Consider making outings into a ritual that can be predicted and eventually seen as enjoyable. You might even pair a not-so-fun errand with a desirable trip. You can hit the bank drive-through window on the way to swimming lessons, for instance. Or stop and get gas every Saturday before going to a favorite hardware store.

- Keep it "in the bag." For situations that require a bit more patience and endurance than your child or children might have, consider keeping a boredom grab bag stashed in your car. You can hand over the entire bag or simply give one item at a time as needed. Items for a seven-year-old child might include a mechanical pencil and notepad, an old nonfunctioning cell phone or PDA, a sheet of stickers, a small brainteaser toy, a little book featuring a favorite thing or character, and a squishy or sensory object. Dollar stores and garage sales are good places to find such treats.

2.10. Adaptations While Traveling

When it comes to planning a trip, families of children with autism have to consider more than which airline has the best price and which theme park will be most fun. In order for everyone in the family to have a satisfying experience away, parents and their children have to carefully choose their destination and activities, method of transport, and lodging. Following are some ideas to make traveling more enjoyable for the entire family:

- Do some previewing for the trip. Show your child photos or Web sites of the destination, let him do research on the hotels and attractions, and suggest he keep a scrapbook of the journey.

- Create a checklist (with pictures, if needed) of necessary supplies and involve your child, if possible, in packing.

- Don't forget essentials such as medications, favorite snack or drink, earplugs or headphones, gum and sensory supports (such as candy or a beanbag), and a comfort item. When traveling by car, keep these out of the trunk and within easy reach of mom or dad. When traveling by plane, be sure these items remain in your carry-on bag.

- Research destinations that are known for their commitment to inclusion or for recognizing the special needs of families with children with autism. Several resorts and cruise lines such as Norwegian, Royal Carribean, Celebrity, and Carnival have made efforts to this end, as have Disney, Universal Orlando, Busch Gardens and Six Flags.

- Book travel, when possible, in the slower season, so that crowds and lines will be less challenging. In other words, Sea World during spring break is probably not the best bet!

- Bring items from home that might increase your child's comfort. Sheets from her own bed might be more comfortable than those in a strange motel and, for some children, so would a familiar cup or bowl.

- For some, no matter what supports you put in place, flying will be difficult, if not seemingly impossible. In these families, driving might be the only option for travel. To make long distances bearable, consider renting a van (with television for the kids, if possible) or even an RV.

- Be sure to bring any of the child's special toys, fidgets, and possessions, and be sure to make them accessible. In other words, don't make the mistake of packing these treasures in the bottom of the suitcase. Put all of these items in the child's backpack, purse, or roller bag and let him keep it near at all times.

- If you are flying, take extra precautions. Bring earplugs or headphones if you have them (those used by business travelers tend to be a bit more sturdy and effective than those available on the plane), and suggest the child wear them during the flight. They will block out extra noise and can be used to play soothing music.

- Traveling always involves big changes in daily routines, so do your best to offer a new schedule with estimated times and activities. Because vacations are so unpredictable, be sure to note "schedule may change" at the bottom of each day's menu of events. (Make sure mom, dad, and siblings also understand and are OK with the "schedule may change" concept!)

- Call ahead to hotels and inquire about amenities so that you can plan for the best possible trip. Consider the needs of your child. Does he enjoy video games? If so, do they have an arcade? Are favorite chain restaurants close to the attractions you will visit?

- Tie travel into a child's passion, fascination, or interest. Safari parks are sure to satisfy those who are crazy about African animals, camping may be bliss to the nature lover, and a budding scientist may be at his best when museum hopping. Consider more than just the themes of the trip, however, when you think of a person's preferences. One family we know had a wonderful trip to Mexico because they got a room overlooking the sea for their ocean-loving son.

- If the child uses pictures to communicate (and even if he doesn't), consider bringing a page of symbols related to travel, transportation, hotels, and vacation. These images can be used to build an illustrated schedule or to simply make communication easier.

- Be sure to leave plenty of time for relaxation, downtime, and preferred activities (such as swimming, surfing the internet, or watching favorite television programs).

2.11. Helping Your Child Learn at Home

Whether you are playing in the backyard, putting toys away, or doing simple chores, opportunities for teaching and learning abound. Following are some ideas to enhance learning at home for your child on the spectrum:

- Make learning a fun part of daily activities. For instance, on a road trip, read the signs as you drive along, talk about any celebrated landmarks, discuss how to calculate your arrival time using distance and speed, and name any heavy equipment you see in construction zones. At bath time you can ask your child to predict whether different toys will sink or float and demonstrate mixing colors using bath paint.

- Use materials your child loves. If your child loves plastic bags, for instance, collect a range of bags from different stores and organizations. Read the text on the bag to your child, fill bags with different objects (such as a bag filled with objects that begin with the letter A and a bag filled with objects that begin with the letter B), make crafts with bags (such as a plastic bag caterpillar), and put the bags into groups or sets (such as blue bags in one pile and white bags in another pile). If the child loves yarn, make letters and numbers with strands, make doll characters to use in play, or teach knitting, if possible.

- Follow your child's lead. If she likes lining up toy soldiers, you can line them up too. Then count them, separate them into groups of two and count by twos, make geometric shapes with them, have them talk about fun math facts, or line them up on a map or a number line.

- Talk and share information, even if your child is nonverbal or does not have reliable and functional communication. Children who cannot talk or express themselves easily can't ask questions like other children do—such as "Why is the sky blue?" or "How do airplanes fly?"—so their loved ones must give them information and share ideas without these cues. If you are taking a walk through your community, you can tell your child about the different types of architecture (such as: "This is a bungalow made mostly of brick. That type of window is called stained glass"). If you are riding in the car, you can talk about the leaves changing colors or the types of clouds in the sky.

- Look for opportunities to learn through chores. Whether you are trying to teach your child to cook a meal for himself or do the family laundry, you can work on academic skills as well. Sorting—whites from darks, shapes of cookie cutters, types of toys—is an early math skill. Measurement—a quarter cup or half a pound—can be taught when cooking. Filling ice trays is an opportunity to teach about the states of matter.

- Read to your child. Some children will love this activity, and you will have no problem getting them to sit, listen, and cuddle. Other children will struggle to engage in this activity as it is usually conducted, so parents will need to make a few adjustments. For instance, if your child doesn't like to come near you when you read, don't put the book away. Watch to see if he or she paces back and forth or stays in the room when you are reading—this may be evidence that the child is listening but unable to sit still during the activity. You might also try using a silly, high-pitched, or cartoonlike voice to draw the child's attention and make the activity seem fun and playful. You can also create a videotape of yourself reading aloud and play the videotapes for your child. So many on the spectrum like watching video and find it less challenging and socially demanding than climbing in dad's lap or sitting shoulder to shoulder. If none of these work (and even if they do) you can also try using books on CD as a way of sharing books with your child. Play them in the car during trips to therapy, while running errands, or on longer car trips.

- Hone communication skills by playing question-and-answer games at dinner. Using Trivial Pursuit cards, cards you make yourself, or books with getting-to-know-you questions, choose a question each evening to ask and answer. Take turns both reading the questions and providing answers. Have all family members participate so your child can get ideas on how to answer and how to involve everyone in a game. If your child needs help staying on topic or being concise, challenge him to answer using only a certain amount of words or provide an answer in a minute or less. For children who communicate using sign language, pictures, or a communication device, give plenty of time and encouragement to communicate, and be sure the questions can be answered with the system the child is using.

- Create a print rich environment in the home. Post weekly menus on the fridge, put labels on dresser drawers, and buy placemats with words or the alphabet on them.

- Find out what the curriculum and standards are for your child's grade or age (available from the teacher, school board, or even by glancing at your district standards online) and look for opportunities to teach and reinforce the content at home. Specifically, you want to find out what students of this age are expected to know and do and then decide how you might help teach this information or determine which pieces of the curriculum are most important and appropriate for your child. If fifth graders are learning the regions of the United States, for instance, you might create a salt and flour map or complete a huge jigsaw puzzle of the country as a family. If you feel that standard is too complex for your child, you might teach him part of it (such as identifying the region you live in). Even if your child has significant disabilities and is nonverbal, you can start introducing him to grade-level content. For instance, using the same example of studying the United States, you can collect brochures from different state tourism bureaus, use placemats featuring the fifty states, and share facts about your own state. Remember that even if your child cannot *show* you what he knows, it doesn't mean he doesn't know it.

- Turn on the closed captioning feature on your television. Many children on the spectrum enjoy seeing the text that matches the words they hear. For some, this may also be a tool for learning to read.

2.12. Advocating for Your Child

Advocacy is about support. When it comes to working with the school system, that support may involve providing resources, helping others see your child's abilities and needs, and sharing the family's and the individual's vision and dreams. Following are some of the ways you can advocate effectively for your child on the spectrum:

- Come prepared. Bring pens and pencils, a folder, and maybe even paper clips or a ministapler to keep materials organized. If you have a hard time remembering what was said or cannot bring your spouse or advocate, you may also want to bring a tape recorder. You might also bring a photo of your child to keep the conversation centered on her.

- Come with ideas. As a parent, you have the right to meaningful participation in the individualized education plan (IEP) meeting. You should, share your vision for your child's education and future, suggest goals for your child's program (bring ideas in writing to make suggestions easier to follow and incorporate), and express concern about suggested goals.

- Approach advocacy with a positive attitude. Go into the meeting expecting a collaborative spirit, an energetic exchange of ideas, and good outcomes for your child.

- Know your value. Be confident about your contributions and your participation. Nobody knows more about your child than you do. You have much to offer the team, and your contributions will be unique and valuable.

- Educate yourself about autism and share what you have learned. Read up on the topic (see Section Five for print and Web resources), attend conferences, if possible, and talk to other families who have children on the spectrum. Bring conference brochures, relevant articles, and ideas for support and teaching to the meetings.

- Learn about your child's rights as they relate to education. In particular, you should familiarize yourself with Public Law 94-142 (PL 94-142) and the child's right to "supports and services" and education in the "least restrictive environment." These terms are important to understand in context. For instance, parents should understand that if their child is included in a general education classroom, a range of the aforementioned supports and services can be used to support that placement (such as integrated occupational therapy, special seating, and teaching strategies). Further, parents should understand that severity of disability does not dictate placement or services: students with severe disabilities can be successfully included in general education classrooms, and students with mild disabilities may qualify for a range of supports.

- Don't go it alone. Bring an advocate to meetings if you need help expressing yourself or understanding jargon or if you feel uncomfortable during meetings. This is often a good idea if for no other reason than to compare notes afterwards, to help ensure that you each heard the same things, and to see if you each made the same interpretation of intentions, body language, and recommendations.

- Get involved. Your level of involvement with the school will increase when you have a child on the spectrum. If you don't already know the principal, the director of special education (or of pupil services), the social worker, the counselors, and the school psychologist, get to know them. If you have the time and the inclination, it can also help your child (and your school) if you get involved in other ways such as joining the PTA, going to school events, and volunteering at the school. Such participation not only helps you and your child feel more involved in the school community but also encourages other students, parents, teachers, and administrators view you in thisk way.

- Advocate and network with advocates. The Autism National Committee and the Autism Society of America, for example, have annual conferences and resource-rich Web sites. In addition, every state has local chapters of the Autism Society of America as well as a number of groups that offer information, education, support groups, technical assistance, and other resources. To find an advocacy group that works for you, identify your primary needs and look for a group that matches those needs. If you are concerned about health issues, look for a group with that interest. If you want to create better vocational opportunities and career counseling in your area, look for groups that are focused on the needs of adolescents and adults. The group may not necessarily be an autism-focused group, of course, so cast a wide net in your search.

- Know your rights. If your child qualifies for special education programs or services, learn about them and remember that you do not have to accept any placements, services, or programs, and you can discontinue a placement, service, or program at any time.

- Stay connected. Ask that regular, short, informal meetings be scheduled with your child's teachers and school therapists. You can actually write these meetings into the IEP. Use this time to simply touch base about the progress your child is making, any areas of concern, and to make sure you and the team members are on the same page. To distinguish these from formal IEP meetings, one family we know calls these WFF meetings—meetings where each team member can get a Warm Fuzzy Feeling that things are on track. In this informal setting, without the stressors inherent in a formal IEP meeting, you may find that you and your child's teachers begin to build real and collaborative relationships around the success of your child. In all likelihood, you will find that much of the real work of creating a meaningful education plan will be done in these meetings, thus paving the way to much more successful annual IEP team meetings.

- Keep good records of work samples, reports, IEPs, evaluations, and assessments. Depending on the needs of your child, these documents may fill an accordion file by the time she leaves school or an entire file cabinet or more. These records will help you chart progress, communicate clearly with your family physician, and ease transitions from year to year.

3

CHECKLISTS FOR TEACHERS

Introduction

Introduction

The following section addresses issues that will be of special interest to the teachers of students on the spectrum. While many of the previous lists in this book—including those in the family section—will be helpful for teachers, this section provides information on topics that are specific to classrooms and schools. We have included, for instance, checklists on dealing with identification, teacher attitudes, one on the specific needs of learners with autism, and a fourth list that deals simply with ways to get more information on autism and students with that label. Other lists in this section deal with the day-to-day needs of teachers, such as supporting school-to-school transitions and classroom-to-classroom transitions, helping students succeed with homework, and addressing passions and fascinations. We also added a list of don'ts for teachers, so that the most common pitfalls can be avoided from the first day of school to the last.

Because teachers will also need to know how to individualize instruction and create responsive curricula, this section contains lists for creating lessons, giving clear directions, providing structure, making whole-class discussions accessible, and creating quality assessments. We have also included two specific lists to help teachers design literacy and mathematics lessons that will be appropriate and appealing to students on the spectrum.

Many educators will also be seeking ideas for positive behavior support in the classroom. Our list on preventing behavior struggles in the classroom will help those looking for ways to keep students calm, relaxed, and feeling supported, and the one on helping students become advocates will provide ideas for preventing difficulties and fostering empowerment. Other lists in this section will help address specific behavior challenges such as student anxiety, perfectionism, and work avoidance.

Finally, in today's diverse and often inclusive classrooms, educators are increasingly seeking strategies for encouraging cooperation, teaching social skills, facilitating friendships, and cultivating a sense of belonging. We have created lists that address these goals. To learn more, see our ideas for building a supportive classroom community, our hints on helping students with autism shine, and our recommendations for creating comfortable and safe classrooms for learners on the spectrum.

Whether you are a teacher, paraprofessional, therapist, psychologist, social worker, or administrator, we hope the following lists will become useful tools in your work.

3.1. What to Do If You Think a Student Is on the Spectrum

It is not the job of a teacher to diagnose autism. Rather, the teacher who suspects a students is on the spectrum should make observations; try a wide range of strategies and techniques to support learning, behavior, or sensory difficulties; and refer the child for an informal or formal evaluation if necessary. Following are the most helpful things you can do before requesting an evaluation:

- Observe. Make mental notes of how the student behaves, interacts, and performs across different environments and contexts. Write down anything you think might ultimately be helpful to a student support team and the family (such as work habits, struggles, and academic needs).

- Talk to colleagues. Ask a teacher from the previous year about his experiences with the student. You can ask the teacher to share any success stories or strategies that work well for the learner. You might also talk to a school social worker, behavior support person, or psychologist to get ideas on approaches you can try.

- Provide assistance. Don't wait for a formal diagnosis or extra help to provide support to a child who needs it. Any child in the classroom who is being bullied, needs academic help, struggles socially, appears anxious, or requires individual attention will need some kind of response, whether or not he qualifies for services or is recognized as having a disability. Use any existing resources you have in the classroom or building to meet such needs. Consider adding support from peers, cross-age tutors (older students in the building), or classroom volunteers and use strategies you have employed for other students with similar needs.

- Try, try, and try again. Implement a range of strategies to support the learner and take note of what does and does not seem to work. You may even want to collect some work samples and informally interview the student to get more information about his perspective, needs, and abilities.

- Pay attention to what is going well. Keep a list of the student's strengths. This information will be very useful as you develop methods to support him or her. It will also be a tool that can be used in any evaluation that may be conducted during the year.
- Consider referral. If you are still concerned after following these suggestions you may want to fill out a referral form and take the case to the student support team.

3.2. Needs of Students with Autism

Students with autism need teachers with open minds and a willingness to learn more than anything else. Following are some of the other things that will help students on the spectrum succeed:

- An inclusive and welcoming school community
- A school team willing to collaborate with the student's parents and private caregivers or therapists to create a learning environment that is as seamless and mutually supportive as possible
- Support and understanding from those in the learning community (such as bus drivers and cafeteria workers)
- Peer support and opportunities to learn from the classroom community
- Clear and precise communication from all adults
- Opportunities to hone communication skills and competencies across the school day
- Opportunities to hone social skills and competencies across the school day
- A school team willing to adapt curriculum, instruction, and assessment as needed
- Opportunities for active and collaborative learning, and lessons that include plenty of visuals, examples, demonstrations, manipulatives, models, and interaction
- Routines that are reasonably stable
- Organized and easy-to-navigate classrooms
- Help with tasks requiring motor planning, such as writing, shoe tying, and playing certain sports or games
- Respect for sensory differences
- Opportunities to make choices and have some control over environment, materials, schedule, and activities

- Opportunities to move to a safe space when feeling overwhelmed (such as a hallway or space in the library or office)
- Opportunities to learn the same thing in various situations and contexts to encourage generalization of skills
- Avoidance of power struggles, arguing, debating, and long verbal explanations
- Educators who focus on strengths, have high expectations, and look for gifts in every student

3.3. Helpful Habits of Mind for Teachers

When teachers begin working with learners on the spectrum, they often have a lot of questions. They want strategies, tips, and help for Monday morning. We believe it is important for teachers to come to the classroom equipped with plenty of ideas for instruction and support, but we also believe that it can be helpful to reflect on beliefs, values, language, and perceptions before diving into the practical how-tos of teaching and learning. Following are some general principles to keep in mind when teaching students on the spectrum:

- Keep your sense of humor. Not only will keeping things in perspective prevent situations from escalating more than necessary, but if you can find the lighter side of a challenging situation, your students may be able to follow your lead do the same.

- See students and their families as experts. Too often students with autism are told about their label, lives, and experiences without having opportunities to tell their own stories and share their own realities. In order for teachers to be successful, they must be curious about and interested in the expertise and experiences of their students and the families of their students. Most families will gratefully welcome your interest in their child's success, and this type of collaboration will undoubtedly help to build a stronger and better-functioning school-home partnership.

- Focus on strengths and goals that have been met. Ask questions about how students have succeeded in the past.

- Don't assume the worst. Realize the student may be trying his best to behave appropriately. Often what looks on the surface like problem behavior is actually a manifestation of a sensory problem, physical discomfort, an inability to communicate effectively, or to understand or perform what is being asked.

- Preserve the dignity of students. Though every teacher undoubtedly wants to protect students and help them build self-respect and self-esteem, these goals are sometimes inadvertently put on the educational back burner during busy classroom days. When students are not achieving or participating, it is often because we have neglected our personal relationships with them. It is frequently in those moments when we pause to listen to our students and learn about who they are and what they need that we do the most to facilitate their learning.

- Look for complexity. Educators must constantly be scouting for student talents and seeking situations that highlight the abilities and support the needs of diverse learners. Teachers of students with autism must believe that students *are* competent, and then they must set the stage for students to perform competently. Teachers looking for competence and complexity in learners should constantly consider the following questions: How can I help this student find success? What prevents me from seeing this student's competence? What helps me see this student's competence more clearly? How does this student learn? How and what can I learn from this student?

- Act as teacher and learner. Schools need ways of bringing learners and teachers together and of becoming communities in which participants learn from each other. Teachers must have ways of renewing themselves and discovering new ideas. Some may prefer to continue learning through professional development seminars or college courses. Others may seek opportunities in their own buildings. For example, one school held a "share-an-idea" coffee gathering every month. Any staff person in the building was invited to attend and to present. Some schools have also instituted book clubs for teachers and other staff members.

- Listen. Teachers who are good listeners often find that students are able to educate them about teaching, learning, disability, ability, and autism, either directly or indirectly. If it is difficult to engage certain learners and to get information from them, look for alternative ways to communicate. You might call the learner at home, send an e-mail or text message, or simply write a note to her in the classroom.

3.4. Learning About Autism

Teachers often crave more information about autism and may assume that they need to crack open old college textbooks or search the Internet to get facts about autism or Asperger syndrome. The truth is that there are as many different ways to learn about autism as there are learners with that label. Following are some ways to learn more about autism and teaching students on the spectrum:

- Ask and listen. If possible, informally interview the student about his or her particular abilities, needs, strengths, and favorites. You might conduct such an interview before the beginning of a school year or simply sit with the student during lunch.

- Learn from people on the spectrum. There are several autobiographies of people with autism that have been published in the last two decades (see Section Five for a list of recommended titles). Use these as a first step in learning about the diversity across people with autism and the many abilities, strengths, and struggles of those on the spectrum. In addition, many people on the spectrum are now on the speaking circuit and are offering workshops for teachers and families around the country. Check out some of these speakers when they come to your area.

- Conduct a home visit. It is time consuming, of course, to visit the home of every student with unique learning needs, but for some learners, such a visit is the best way to see what the individual knows and can do. Many students, especially those with more moderate and significant disabilities, shine the most when they are around people, materials, and surroundings that are familiar. This visit can be used to introduce yourself, talk to the family, observe the student, familiarize yourself with any adaptive equipment or special materials the individual uses, or even just to socialize with the learner and make him feel more comfortable with you and with school.

- Look for support and information from parent groups. Families of those on the spectrum are a great resource and are often more than willing to share their stories and exchange ideas. You can find these groups in almost any community, and they very often open their events and meetings to teachers, community workers, and others interested in learning more about autism.

- Reach out. Many autism-related organizations sponsor resource fairs, speakers on various topics, and workshops throughout the year. The Autism Society of America, for example, has several chapters in each state. Some of these are very small and offer only outreach or information, but others sponsor conferences and other learning opportunities.

- Chat with colleagues. Talk to other teachers who have successfully educated students with diverse needs and abilities in an inclusive classroom. If the student has previously been educated in a general education classroom, it might be helpful to talk to the teachers who supported the student in that situation. Teachers who have specific teaching roles might find it helpful to talk to others who share their responsibilities. For instance, a science teacher might find it very helpful to talk to the student's previous science teacher, and the student's speech therapist might want to talk to the student's previous therapists.

- If you have many students with autism in your classes or if you have a special interest in the needs of these learners, you might want to take a course on teaching those with autism. These courses are more available than ever before and can be found at community colleges and universities alike. Some courses are also offered in other formats (such as webinars and distance learning) and are often designed to meet the needs of busy professionals. The special education or student support services office of your school district will likely have information on the availability of offerings in your area. For starters, visit www.tash.org for a list of current low-cost webinars. Although not all of these are specifically on autism, most of them relate to teaching people with disabilities.

- Observe the student in her current classroom setting. This type of observation should focus on the student's successes: What can this student do well? Where is she strong? What has worked to create success for the student? The observing teacher might also record questions for the student's current teacher.

- Surf the net. Visit various websites not only to learn about autism but to chat with other teachers and get ideas and inspiration. See Section 5 for websites we recommend including Paula's site (www.paulakluth.com) which has a lot of teacher-tested ideas for K–12 classrooms.

3.5. Encouraging Self-Advocacy

Teachers may not always think of themselves as advocates, but if students with autism are going to be successful, they need educators who support them and help them feel and act empowered. Following are some effective ways to encourage self-advocacy for students on the spectrum:

- Define advocacy and self-advocacy for students and share the importance of learning related skills such as creating a vision for oneself, defining abilities and struggles, and communicating wants and needs.

- Serve as an advocate yourself. In many cases, teachers who have students with disabilities in their classrooms become responsible for teaching other educators about these disabilities and how to support these learners. Be sure that in all of your conversations you talk about students in positive and respectful ways. Help your student secure the services he or she needs, and help others provide necessary supports. Depending on the age of the student, it may be appropriate to tell the learner about how you advocate for students, what strategies you use, and why you feel advocacy is important.

- Teach self-advocacy strategies that work with the individual's learning style, and provide the person choices for gathering information, sharing knowledge, and teaching others. A young child who wants peers to know about his autism label and related needs might be asked if he wants to present the information formally to the class or just tell a few classmates. If he wants to present the information formally, you might give him the option of writing an All About Me book and reading it to peers, preparing a PowerPoint presentation to share, or simply telling others about this characteristic at a time when other students are sharing information (such as during a Student of the Week presentation).

- Point the student in the right direction. Identify good resources for learning about advocacy such as the Internet, local support groups, and useful books and guides. In some cases, it might also be appropriate to suggest that the learner attend local, regional, or national conferences where she can hear other self-advocates present. Some local chapters of the Autism Society of America or other advocacy organizations may also sponsor support groups or social-skills groups where the student can meet others on the spectrum and work to gain social competency and self-confidence.

- Create an advocacy notebook with the individual. Encourage him to collect materials related to his needs and abilities. A notebook might contain information about autism, lists of favorite books, movies, or resources on the topic, pamphlets from conferences attended, artifacts from any advocacy groups he belongs to, or any materials the student has created related to his life on the spectrum.

- Work with the student to create her own self-advocacy products. Not all learners will be able to represent themselves in IEP meetings or express to teachers what they can do, what they need, and how they feel. Some students simply do not have the confidence or skills to do these things, whereas others may be too young or have yet to learn the required communication skills. For these students, it may be appropriate to help them construct a personal portfolio, a short video, a pamphlet, a PowerPoint presentation, a Web site, or even a simple "business card" that can be given to new teachers and other staff members. Nonverbal students might simply create a short handout to bring to IEP meetings or to give to new staff members. This handout might consist of a few photographs demonstrating favorite activities and areas of strength; teachers and parents can add ideas for useful supports.

3.6. Addressing Student Fascinations and Passions in the Classroom

Whether your students loves sharks, heavy equipment, sewers, game shows, or Ireland, their fascinations can be used in the classroom and integrated into curriculum and instruction. Following are some ways to address the fascinations of your students on the spectrum:

- Consider changing some of your terminology. Most textbooks, professionals, and experts refer to fascinations and passions as "obsessions" or even "stims." Using language that is softer and more generous, including words and phrases such as "passions," "favorites," "special interests," "loves" or "areas of expertise," may help teachers see student favorites as tools instead of as nuisances.

- Think about your lessons. Any interest can be used as part of the K–12 curricula. A student who loves trains might be asked to write a story about riding on a caboose (language arts), research different railroads on the Internet (computers and research), calculate the distances of various U.S. railway routes (mathematics), compare and contrast different kinds of engines, such as steam and diesel-electric (science), or do an independent research project on ground transportation in the United States (social studies). Or instead of starting the brainstorming process from the point of the interest area, you might begin by looking at the curriculum for any subject and generate ideas that way. As you scan the science curriculum for seventh grade and see lessons on technology, mass, or force, consider ways you can incorporate a child's interest in elevators into some of the upcoming lessons on these topics.

- Look for ways to use the individual's interest to enrich learning in the classroom. Are there any ways for a student to teach other learners about his interest during upcoming lessons? Could a child who loves whales talk about these animals during a unit on oceans? Could a student who loves maps teach a few cartography skills to peers during social studies?

- Use fascinations to encourage socializing and chitchat. Students with autism—particularly those with Asperger syndrome and others who have reliable communication—are often accused of having poor social skills and specifically of being unable to engage in small talk successfully. Students may struggle with this skill because they have a hard time figuring out how to enter a conversation or simply because they may not feel comfortable participating in a conversation that does not pertain to subjects they know well. Encouraging students to join conversations by chatting about their favorites is one way to ease fears, anxieties, and doubts in this area. Of course, it can be a problem if the student talks only about her passions when engaged in small talk, but we feel that if the learner is taught to monitor things like how long she is talking about the passion or if she has created spaces to take turns in the conversation, fascinations can be a perfectly appropriate topic for chitchat with acquaintances and strangers alike. This concept is important because if the student does not use her area of expertise as a way into the conversation, she may not enter it at all.

- Allow extra-credit opportunities related to interests. If a student needs to bring grades up or spend more time on content or skills that have been challenging, you could pair the student's passion with a proposed extra-credit project. If the student needs more work on reading fluency, ask him to create or find short books on his favorite subject area and create opportunities for him to read these books to several of the younger students in the school.

- Address a struggle with a strength. Use the interest to teach unfamiliar or difficult content. Use a passion for football, for instance, to teach statistics in mathematics.

- Use the interest to help a learner through a challenging moment. For instance, you might let a student have a favorite object during a fire drill or discuss her love of mythology when she is feeling stress over a change in the schedule.

- Help students shine. Students with autism labels may want to use their passion or fascination to show off their talents and demonstrate to others the ways in which they are smart. This may be especially important for learners who have been seen or labeled as challenging or difficult. The debate team might be a vehicle for those who want structured ways to share what they know. Clubs are another possibility. A student who is an expert problem-solver might want to join the Math Olympiad, and the learner who loves politics would thrive in the Model UN.

- Use fascinations as a springboard. Teachers can also use fascinations to connect students to new interests and areas of study. A student who loves talking about the weather might be asked to read about the weather in the daily newspaper and then coaxed into glancing at stock quotes, baseball scores, or local election coverage as well. A student with a fascination with the flags of various countries might be encouraged to prepare a bulletin board every couple of weeks with the flag of a different nation and include a list of facts about that country and its people, products, or geography. A student with an interest in math might be asked to prepare a series of brief reports on famous mathematicians and thereby work toward building an interest in history as well. If these sorts of rituals are repeated over time, the individual may expand his areas of interest as well as learn new standards-based concepts and information.

3.7. Supporting Students Who Seek Perfection

Many learners on the spectrum struggle with perfectionism. This characteristic will manifest itself differently in different students. Some may want to revise their work over and over again. Others will be afraid to try new things. Still others may become overwhelmed by the need to continually clean or organize materials. Following are some ways to support students on the spectrum who seek perfection:

- Focus on the positive. Try not to directly address things the learner does improperly or incorrectly. It may be more effective to use encouraging or positive language instead and to demonstrate what should be done. For example, instead of telling a young child he has written a word incorrectly, you might say, "Let's check our dictionary to see if all our words are spelled correctly."

- Talk about yourself. All learners will profit from teachers who talk about their own learning style, preferences, and challenges, so when you struggle with learning something or make an error, tell students about it. It can be helpful to share both big mistakes (such as forgetting to attend an important meeting) and little ones (such as writing the wrong answer on the board) and to explicitly discuss how you deal with them (such as repeating a mantra, fixing the problem, or making light of the situation).

- Encourage all students to "just try" and to take risks. Create a safe classroom environment where students are encouraged to explore new skills and experiences. Discuss risk taking in the course of curriculum as well. During a lesson on Abraham Lincoln, for instance, a teacher might bring up his many setbacks and his political losses, as well as his victories.

- Talk to the student about setting reasonable goals. Have her practice goal setting often. For instance, ask her to set a goal for a score on a test or on the number of days she can get to the classroom on time during the course of a month.

- Teach students to set time limits for projects or other types of work. Have the student practice stopping work when the timer goes off. Some students may even enjoy learning this skill in some kind of game format where you celebrate or reward each time he stops working "at the bell." Teach the learner eventually to assign his own cutoff times, maximum amount of rewrites, or number of attempts.

- Try teaching a mantra (possibly by making an index card with the mantra printed on the card) about letting go or being imperfect, and teach students to repeat the phrase in times of stress (such as "Nobody's perfect" or "At least I tried" or "Risk is its own reward").

3.8. Supporting Students Who Resist or Refuse to Do Work

Getting started, transitioning, taking risks, and participating in new and unfamiliar activities can all be challenges for those on the spectrum. Students may react to these challenges by "freezing" or panicking, or by refusing to engage or respond. Following are some ways to sensitively support students on the spectrum who resist doing work:

- Examine any underlying reason for the resistance. Could the student be struggling to understand what needs to be done? Does she have the necessary skills to perform the requested task? Is she experiencing sensory problems that are interfering with getting work done?

- Use a "first-then" board. On the left-hand side draw a picture or write a description of the task that needs to be addressed first (such as completing the fractions worksheet). On the right-hand side, draw a picture of the task or activity that the learner can engage in after the first activity is complete (such as playing a race car game on the computer).

- Share the reason. Some students on the spectrum may resist activities that don't make sense or seem to have a purpose. Sharing the "why" of the activity may work for some students. For instance, a child who does not want to practice the dialogue from the class play over and over again (because he has already read the play once) might need more information on what rehearsal is and why actors practice. You might even give him a new goal each time so he feels the experience is novel on each occasion.

- Use a special interest or area of expertise to motivate and interest the learner. If she won't (or can't) work on the vocabulary words you have assigned her to define, tie them to her interest area. For instance, a child who loves Paula

Dean, the TV cooking phenomenon, was allowed to write all of her vocabulary words and definitions on recipe cards instead of in a notebook.

- Start small. If the student constantly refuses to perform a particular task, give him the opportunity to do it for a very short period. Over time, gradually increase the period he engages in the task.

- Teach them how they learn. Try giving choices that might empower the student and help her explore her learning preferences, such as "Do you want to do this sitting at your desk or do you want to do it sitting on the floor?" or "Do you want to write a response or draw one?"

- Try starting the task or activity with or for the learner. For instance, if the individual won't (or can't) start writing an assigned essay, the teacher might write the first sentence, work together with the student to write the first sentence, or serve as a scribe as the student shares a few sentences verbally.

- Help the student learn from others. The learner may be very reluctant to try new things, begin things that just seem too difficult, or engage in activities that feel risky. Having another student share positive experiences about the activity can be comforting to some. Better yet, have students regularly share successes with one another and highlight those that caused unease for the person at some stage or those that required hard work.

3.9. Helping Students Cope with Anxiety

Not all students with autism struggle with anxiety, but many do. Unfortunately, not all learners understand their anxiety or they are unable to communicate effectively about it, so an anxious student can look like a defiant, noncompliant, inattentive, or disengaged student. Teachers therefore need to consider anxiety as a root when they see such behaviors, so that supports can be put in place. Following are some ways to help students on the spectrum deal with anxiety:

- Make self-awareness a goal for learners. Help them name and interpret emotions, and encourage them to share feelings and difficulties with staff members or trusted peers. Make it an ongoing practice to introduce new vocabulary (such as miserable, dejected, elated, melancholy, satisfied) to students so they can become better and better at expressing precisely how they feel.

- Identify cues. Ask the student's family about the individual's "stress signals." For instance, does he show changes in posture, tone of voice, or movements when he is becoming frustrated, upset, or tense?

- Address early signs. If a student is showing signals that he is feeling anxious (and especially if his anxiety seems to be escalating), talk to him about what you see. You might say, "I can hear you whispering to yourself, Jon. Do you need something? Can I help you?"

- Teach the student how to signal or verbally communicate distress. For example, you might teach him a signal that means "I need a break" (something as simple as putting an eraser on the desk can work well and be unobtrusive) or provide special "pass" cards that can be handed to the teacher when he is feeling overloaded and needs to leave the classroom.

- Suggest the common approaches that we all use to cope with stress like listening to a bit of music, taking a short walk, using visualization, and engaging in positive self-talk.

- Give predictable breaks throughout the day, if needed. Make sure, however, that the break activities are age-appropriate and carefully managed so that learners have the comfort they need, but as much continuity in the school day as possible.

- Talk, share, and offer support to the family. Some students will perform well during the school day, but unravel the moment they walk through their front door. This tendency to come undone at home (a safe space) rather than at school is reported often by many on the autism spectrum. For this reason, there must be regular lines of communication between parents and teachers so that supports at school can be adjusted to reduce any struggles at home.

- Encourage connection, conversation, and community. At the end of particularly stressful days, allow for a short debriefing session with a social worker, teacher, or an understanding peer. In these sessions, let the student explain what happened, but spend most of the time developing strategies for avoiding these difficulties in future.

3.10. Building a Supportive Classroom Community

It will be a challenge for students to hone social skills if their classroom is not a safe and welcoming place to play, learn, and interact. Following are some ways to build a more supportive classroom community for your students on the spectrum:

- Ask for preferences. Ask students on the autism spectrum whether (and, if so, how) they want to share information with other students about their label. Some may want to keep the information private, whereas others may be eager to talk about their differences.

- Communicate your philosophy to all students. From the first day of school to the last, it is important that students understand that they won't all get the same treatment from you and that this differentiation of expectation, attention, instruction, and even curriculum is necessary and appropriate. You can point out that students with vision problems may sit near the front of the room, those who have sensory challenges may use fidget toys or have different seating, and those who need extra challenge on certain assignments may be asked to use different materials. When the teacher consistently responds to all learners as individuals, students are far less likely to be concerned about why some students have or do certain things and others do not.

- Create a democracy. No matter which grade level you teach, it can be helpful to construct your class rules *with* your students instead of *for* them. Students who have a say in the government of the classroom are more likely to respect rules and policies.

- Ban bullying. Make it clear that name calling, teasing, and harassment are not acceptable in the classroom. Take it a step further and ask students to talk about their experiences in unsafe learning spaces. Ask them for ideas on keeping the classroom safe and comfortable for all.

- Talk to all students about the expectations for collaborative work. Provide reminders about what collaboration and cooperation look like (such as materials being shared and everyone getting a turn) and sound like (such as "Can I have a turn?" or "What do you think?").

- Use role-play to demonstrate cooperation. Bring a few students forward to role-play a joint task such as making a snack. Explain that the purpose is to help us think about what it means to work together. As the volunteers work together to count out the granola bars and pour the juice, narrate each step of the task. Point out the different ways the students help one another, get support, and communicate. If you have very specific behaviors you want to teach or illustrate, you can give the students a script for the role-play.

- Create opportunities for team building. Use cooperative games, active learning, and community-building activities to encourage students to get and give support and learn from one another. Students will feel more comfortable asking for help and providing assistance when they have had opportunities to interact with others across situations and activities.

- Come together through curriculum. Look for ways for all students to share their needs, struggles, and gifts through structures such as icebreakers, games, reflective writing, art, journaling, book clubs, or storytelling. A student who is reluctant to discuss his need for sameness and order might find the courage to speak out if he is discussing a character with similar traits in a novel.

- Encourage everyone to share their uniqueness. Consider having students share their personal stories as a way of creating connections throughout the classroom. You might ask learners to write autobiographies, create documentaries of their lives, serve as the Student of the Week, or simply fill out All About Me worksheets that can be posted on a bulletin board.

- Too often students with autism receive support or services without getting opportunities to give the same. Service learning projects such as cleaning up a parks, tutoring younger children, or making care packages for veterans can strengthen your classroom community and help all learners serve as helpers.

3.11. Creating a Comfortable Classroom

Students with autism will have a hard time focusing and learning if they are not comfortable. Use of space and classroom seating, lighting, sounds, and smells all need to be considered in planning a learning environment for learners on the spectrum. The suggestions that follow can help make your classroom more safe and welcoming for students on the spectrum.

Space

- Create quiet study areas. In most schools, spare classrooms do not exist, but if they do an administrator might be willing to convert some space into a full-day quiet study area that any student can access. In crowded schools, teachers might work with the school librarian or study hall monitor to create a space just for studying or projects. Or a few chairs and even a small table might be set up in the hallway (if fire code regulations permit) for any student who needs a break from the bustle of the classroom.

- Seek spaces for active learning. Whereas many students have the need for quiet, others need movement, activity, and interaction. A student who cannot sit at a desk or keep a low voice in a classroom can participate by working on some of the course material in a different environment with a few classmates or on a related lesson in a community environment with a small group.

- Create different areas for different activities. For instance, a high school teacher might have an area that is just for storage and teacher materials, a small library area, and an activity table. An elementary school teacher could have a puppet show theater and drama center, a reading corner, and a whole-class gathering place. When possible, areas can be sectioned off (using furniture, masking tape, or by painting the floor different colors) to help students understand how spaces are to be used.

- Keep high-traffic areas free of congestion, if possible. The pencil sharpener, classroom library, and supply cabinet should be kept in separate areas and should be kept in places least likely to interfere with class functioning and activity or at least away from the students who get distracted the most easily. A student with autism may become frustrated if students are constantly walking past her desk or crossing in front of a chalkboard she is trying to read.

Seating

- Make it cozy. Some teachers like adapt the environment by installing a carpet sample in one area of the classroom or by putting a few armchairs in a special part of the room. We know of a high school teacher who clustered student desks together in groups of four and cleared nearly half the classroom for a community area. This section of the room contained an old coffee table, two loveseats, and a huge upholstered footstool. Similarly, an elementary classroom we have visited has a cozy learning space filled with pillows, carpet squares, and stuffed toys.
- Give them the floor! Some students may prefer to sit on the floor for some part of the day. These students can work on clipboards or use lap desks.
- Rocking chairs are a nice supplement to any K–12 classroom. Students with and without autism will enjoy having an occasional opportunity to rock and read, rock and work, or rock and relax.
- Provide a cushion. Tie-on chair cushions (available at discount stores) are one of the easiest seating adaptations that can be offered to any student in the classroom. Because the cost is low, you might consider getting one for every chair in your classroom. Students with and without sensory problems appreciate them and may profit from their use.

- Got furniture? If space permits, a small couch, loveseat, or armchair can make a classroom feel more familiar, welcoming, and comfortable.

- Keep looking for new options. In addition to the other suggestions already offered, try reading pillows, exercise mats, physio balls, lawn furniture, director chairs, footstools, and large floor pillows and keep looking for more.

Lighting

- Forgo fluorescents if you can. Fluorescent lighting can affect learning, behavior, and the comfort level of students with autism. To determine whether or not fluorescent lights are problematic for students in your classroom, turn off the overhead lights for a day to see if the change seems to affect any of your students. If the lighting does seem to be a concern for someone, you may need to replace fluorescents with incandescent bulbs or experiment with different ways of using light.

- Try lower levels of light, if possible.

- Use upward-projecting rather than downward-projecting lighting.

- Experiment with different types of lighting. Turn on the front bank of lights, but not the back, or turn on alternating banks of lights. In one classroom, teachers strung white holiday lights around their whiteboards and plugged night-lights into different sockets around the room to give the classroom a more peaceful feeling.

- Try different colors of light. Experiment with a pink bulb in one area of the room, for instance.

- Try colored overlays. Some students find it particularly difficult to use white paper under fluorescent lights. Students may be bothered by the glare from the paper.

- Suggest shades. Sunglasses can be worn during recess or can even be tried indoors (especially near fluorescent lighting). Wearing a baseball cap or visor can also help students avoid direct exposure to light.

- Move the student's seat. Sometimes the problem is not the lights themselves, but the reflection of light on a wall or other surface.

- Talk to the custodian. Fluorescent bulbs tend to flicker more as they age. If you must use fluorescent lights, use the newest bulbs possible.

- Is it the light or the sound? Some students are more distracted by the sound than the sight of fluorescent lighting. In these cases, the student may want to use earplugs while studying. In other instances, simply moving the student farther away from the noise may help.

- Go natural! Teachers might also try simply seating the learner with autism as close to the windows as possible. If enough natural light comes into the classroom, the bank of lights over the learner's seat can be shut off.

Sounds

- Assess difficulties. Some students with autism will not only struggle with sounds most of us view as annoying (such as car alarms or sandpaper on wood), but may also react negatively to sounds most of us filter out or even sounds many of us find pleasing. Students might also react negatively to a sound that most find pleasant while failing to react at all to the banging of a door or the scream of a child.

- Investigate. One of the ways teachers can help students cope with sounds is to simply talk to families about which sounds are hardest for the individual. Once a disturbing sound has been identified, the best way to help may involve moving her as far away as possible from the sound source, removing the sound source, changing the sound in some way (such as replacing the ring tone for the teacher's phone), or altering the student's environment (such as changing her English class from one end of the building to another to avoid being near the stairwell).

- Try earplugs or headphones for some activities or for use in some parts of the school building (such as the gym). Realize that you may need to try a whole range of options before you find one that works for your student. Some learners will wear ear buds and others will only use headsets with foam covering.

- Whisper. Use a soft voice when possible. It is in fact easier for many learners on the spectrum to catch quiet voices, so instead of shouting to get a student's attention, try dropping the volume of your voice.

- Reduce classroom noise. Echoes and noise can be reduced by installing carpeting or using carpet remnants. A cheaper solution is to cut open tennis balls and place them on the bottoms of chair and desk legs; this adaptation muffles the scraping sounds created when furniture is shuffled around (ask your local health spa or tennis club for donations).

- Can the sound be changed? For instance, if a student cringes when he hears clapping, students could develop another system of appreciation for student presentations, birthday celebrations, and assemblies. If whistles hurt a student's ears, the physical education teacher might agree to use a megaphone, music, or hand signal to start and stop activities.

- Prepare the student for the sound. If the teacher knows the school bell is about to ring, the student can be cued to plug his ears or simply told to get ready. Or you can note some of these unpleasant sounds (those that occur regularly, anyway) on his daily schedule, so he can mentally prepare for them.

- Allow students to listen to soft music using headsets in noisy or chaotic environments or play soft music for all students (such as classical or environmental music).
- Look for coping strategies. Many students have effective ways of dealing with problematic sounds. Some learners, for example, will concentrate on an object or scribble on paper when they are bothered by sounds. Pay attention to these strategies and avoid interfering with them, if possible. Although a student's coping mechanisms may not be apparent to all, teachers should be open to the possibility that behaviors such as hand flapping and finger flicking may be helpful to the learner, so preventing the student from engaging in these behaviors may cause him more strife.

Smells

- Minimize spraying, misting, and dabbing. Many individuals with autism report that perfume and other personal products cause problems. If a student seems to avoid a particular person or if she will interact with that person only occasionally, it is possible that the student may be reacting to that person's perfume, lotion, hair gel, aftershave, cologne, or shampoo. If a student is very sensitive to these types of smells, teachers and other professionals working in the classroom should avoid scented products as much as possible. In secondary schools, teachers may even want to talk to the classroom community about this issue. Students in the class may be willing to limit the use of certain health and beauty items in order to make their classmate more comfortable.
- Food smells are incredibly distracting for some students with autism. If you have a student who is especially sensitive, you may need to make a few changes. Keeping birthday and holiday treats out of the classroom before parties and seating a child away from the kitchen and the cafeteria are two ways this sensory difference can be addressed. Be aware that

scented markers, books, and stickers (which usually have fruit, candy, or nature fragrances) may also be problematic for some students.

- Air it out. In rooms that have strong smells (such as the art room, cafeteria, or science lab), students can be seated near the door or near an open window. Or provide the student a small personal fan to minimize the impact of the smell.

- Get rid of it. If a student is suffering because of the smell of a classroom pet, a science experiment, or a musty stack of books, you should look for a new home for the source of the offending odor. A pet could be moved to the library, the experiment could be put in a neighboring classroom, and the books can be stored in a closet.

3.12. Giving Clear Directions in the Classroom

Some students on the spectrum have difficulties understanding complex tasks. Others struggle to comprehend verbal directions in general. No matter what your student's difficulty, the following ideas will help you communicate more clearly and give directions more effectively:

- Show and tell when possible. This is especially critical if there are more than two steps to the directions. In these cases, write a step-by-step list on the board so learners can follow along without missing critical information. Add icons or pictures to directions for those who may need more visual support.

- Avoid overloading the student with verbal instructions. Give one instruction at a time and allow the student sufficient time to process and respond to the request.

- For longer processes, consider creating a checklist with the steps listed next to boxes that can be marked off as the student completes them.

- Be as clear as possible. Do not give directions or information in ways that may appear vague or in words that can be easily misinterpreted. For instance, it is better to say, "Please take all the papers off of your desk and put them into your blue folders" than to say "Clear your desktop." Likewise, asking "Can you stop fooling around and get your work done?" is not nearly as direct as "Put your game away and finish the last two problems."

- Avoid figurative language. Many learners on the spectrum struggle to understand devices like metaphors ("This assignment is a bear"), similes ("You are as slow as molasses in January"), and hyperbole ("I've asked you a hundred times to finish that") and will comprehend better when you use language that is plain and straightforward.

- Show examples when appropriate. If you want students to fold their paper in half "the long way," it is best to hold up an example of a sheet of paper with a vertical crease. If you are assigning term papers, leave several out on a table so students can browse through them and use them as templates for their own work.

- Check for understanding. If you are concerned that a student does not understand your directions, ask her to repeat them back to you.

- Wait. Do not give directions during a chaotic time in the classroom. Make sure students are quiet and they are not distracted.

3.13. Providing Structure in the Classroom

Most learners on the spectrum will be able to do their best work when the classroom is organized, materials are easy to find and store, and expectations are consistently outlined and communicated. Following are a variety of ways to provide more structure in the classroom for your students on the spectrum:

- Create routines that are as predictable as possible.
- Try to communicate clear beginning and ending points of activities and lessons.
- Structure units as predictably as you can. For instance, all science units might begin with a preview or outline, followed by some clear objectives, and an introductory lab or experiment.
- Create daily and weekly rituals that all students can look forward to (such as a cooperative game on Friday afternoons).
- Break assignments into meaningful chunks (for example, "First pick an inventor to study. Then find one book in the library about him or her. After you have read the book, see Ms. Hurly to discuss it.")
- Provide a daily schedule on the board (but don't forget to add a reminder at the bottom that indicates "the schedule may change") and provide a personal schedule to students who need to have access to this information all day long. Be sure to update the schedule as changes arise.
- Keep it clean. One way to support learners with autism is to avoid visual clutter. Neatly organize work areas and, when possible, add easy-to-read labels and containers. Even if you teach high school, it will be helpful to students with autism if your classroom resembles a kindergarten classroom when it comes to organization. For instance, a geometry teacher

might have a cart with plastic bins clearly labeled "protractors," "compasses," "extra pencils," and "Geoboards."

- Ask students to be especially conscientious about keeping the classroom neat and about storing their materials in their desks and lockers. And offer students suggestions for keeping things orderly. For instance, instead of asking all students to clear their desks for a test, say "put your notebooks right under your desk." You might also give some ideas on how they might organize desktops, lockers, cubby holes, or backpacks (for example, "Keep your protractor in your pencil bag and only in your pencil bag; then you will always know where to find it").

- Put them to work. In order to make the maintenance of the classroom as easy as possible, you can give all students classroom jobs. For instance, a few students can be responsible for keeping bookcases orderly. Such an activity can even be parlayed into an academic learning experience. Younger students can practice alphabetizing and older students can either learn the Dewey Decimal System or create their own system of categorization. Students can also be responsible for caring for plants, keeping the pencil jar stocked, cleaning chalkboards, organizing bulletin boards, keeping portfolios tidy, straightening tables, clearing out the "work to return" basket, putting new data or information up on the whiteboard or chalkboard, and keeping desks orderly and floors neat.

- Create a cubicle. For those who get too distracted by the sights around them, teachers can construct study carrels from cardboard. A large piece of cardboard (about a foot and a half tall) folded into thirds can be placed on the student's desk to shield him from other students, from classroom materials, and from visual information around the room. Because these carrels are easy and inexpensive to construct, a teacher can make them available to any student in the classroom. Another option is to bring one or two study carrels (the type often found in college libraries) into the classroom and let any student work in the sheltered space when privacy or some focused study is needed.

- Create a desk map so that students can find and replace items independently. Simply draw a map of all items in the desk on a small index card or on a sheet of paper and tape it to the top of the student's desk or attach it to the inside "ceiling" of the desktop. A similar type of map can be created for the classroom in general, for a student's locker, or even for a school bag.

- Keep important information posted clearly. You might keep a calendar, a clock, and a daily schedule in one information area of the classroom or example. Students of any age can be held responsible for writing the date daily, changing the calendar when needed, and even writing out the schedule and other information each morning (such as current weather, stock quotes, "on this day in history," or a poem of the day).

- Do it by the book. Write and make available instruction manuals for different parts of the room (such as how to check a book out of the classroom library) or different activities (such as how to stretch before exercising).

3.14. Creating Lessons with Students with Autism in Mind

Setting clear goals, giving multimodal presentations, encouraging interaction, and using varied teaching materials are just a few of the ways that lessons can be more appealing and interesting to a wider range of students, including those with autism. Following are some specific ideas for creating appropriate lessons for your students on the spectrum:

- When possible, provide an outline or objectives of what you are covering or discussing. You may even want to write the objectives on the board so that students can verify that they learned (or were at least exposed to) the content the teacher intended to teach.

- When possible, use more than one mode of output. If you are talking or lecturing, use PowerPoint slides or overhead notes so students can follow along as you hit the main points. If you coteach or have a paraprofessional in the classroom, that person might take notes while you speak or sketch ideas on a concept map while you give examples and lead a discussion.

- Consider different ways learners might participate in the lesson. If you are asking students to do a "quick write," have you offered assistive technology to those learners who struggle with pencil-and-paper tasks? If you are going to structure a whole-class discussion, will augmentative and alternative communication be available to those who use it?

- Try to address a few different learning styles or intelligences in each lesson. For instance, you might begin the period by showing a movie clip (to engage the visual learners), follow it with small-group skits (to interest those who are kinesthetic), and end with a minilecture (to honor those who are verbal-linguistic).

- Use visuals such as pictures, movies, photographs, graphic organizers, and models when presenting lessons, especially when the content is abstract or new to the student.

- Let them move, talk, share, and interact. Be sure to limit the amount of time you lecture to students. About every twelve to twenty minutes you will want to vary the learning state and lesson format. You might ask students to turn and talk to one another, chant some piece of content, or draw collaborative pictures in response to a lecture.

- Infuse lessons with music. Playing different songs and styles of music can give the teacher an opportunity to expand the experiences of learners, change the energy of the classroom, and inspire and interest students. Music can be used in transitions (when moving from whole-class instruction to small groups) or as a cue for certain behaviors or activities (playing quiz show–type music while students are brainstorming in small groups). Some teachers also use music as part of the curriculum. For instance, a high school teacher might play the song "We Shall Overcome" as part of a unit on the U.S. Civil Rights Movement.

- When possible, make learning active and experiential. For instance, teach the length of a mile by having the class walk that distance together. Teach about fusion and fission by having students move away from each other and then huddle into a small cluster.

- Coteach when possible. Look for opportunities for special education and general education collaboration. Create lessons in which teachers share roles and support learning in a variety of ways. For instance, two teachers could teach together at the helm of a classroom, one teacher could teach a lesson while the other floats and supports the classroom, teachers could split the class into two groups with each teacher providing instruction for a smaller group, or two teachers can facilitate learning during a stations or centers-based lesson. This variety of models helps both teachers expand their strategies while providing opportunities for students with autism to learn from peers and hone social and communication skills.

3.15. Creating More Accessible Whole-Class Discussions and Lectures

Many learners have difficulty staying focused and participating in a whole-class format. This doesn't necessarily mean that these individuals cannot be successful in whole-class lessons, but it might mean that some adaptations to the structure may be necessary. Following are some ways to make discussions and lectures more accessible to your students on the spectrum:

- Location, location, location. Make sure that the student on the spectrum is sitting in a place where he can easily see you and any materials you are presenting. Some on the spectrum rely very heavily on visual supports for learning.

- Get them moving. All students—those with and without autism—are more likely to stay connected to the lesson if you give them opportunities to move, share, and interact. Instead of asking, "Who can tell me the answer?" and calling on one or two students to share information, have students share answers with a partner or have students stand if they think they know the answer.

- Engineer the student's participation. Be sure to structure a way for the learner with autism to contribute if she is unlikely to do so without support. You might begin the discussion with a question or topic the learner knows well, preteach some of the content to prepare the student, or allow the individual to provide a contribution in some alternative way (such as by creating a graphic organizer for the discussion, taking notes for the class on the chalkboard, or asking a question instead of answering one).

- Let them get fidgety. If the whole class lesson will be longer than ten or fifteen minutes, consider offering the student a choice of "fidget supports" or sensory objects (such as a Koosh ball, twisty pencils, or a weighted shoulder snake).

- Integrate technology. PowerPoint software, for instance, is a powerful and dynamic teaching tool that can serve as a visual support for lectures and whole-class discussions. It is also easy to create printed sets of notes from PowerPoint; these can be used as study guides or given to students before lectures so that they can follow along as each point is presented.

- Structure appropriate and respectful interactions. If you have students who occasionally dominate group discussions, you may want to put structures in place to encourage equitable participation. For instance, you might give every student two poker chips to begin the discussion; each participant then hands the teacher a chip when he offers a comment or asks a question. When students are out of chips, they can't add additional comments to the discussion until everyone else is also out of chips. You can also give a particularly chatty student an opportunity to track comments or questions on an AlphaSmart device or in a notebook for the purpose of sharing with a teacher at a later time.

3.16. Creating Assessments Appropriate for Students with Autism

Assessment can certainly cause problems for many on the spectrum because of challenges ranging from frustration with handwriting to stress over the unfamiliar format of a quiz. Tests, exams, and final projects do not need to be dreaded or even stress-filled, however. Consider the following suggestions for making assessments easier and more successful for students on the spectrum:

- Create an optimal environment. Students may find testing conditions hard on their sensory systems. Test days often exacerbate sensory issues, because they require teachers to use the most formal classroom climate and environment (such as bright lights and all students in desks sitting in rows). It may also be difficult for students with autism spectrum labels to sit still and quietly for long periods of time, as is often required during tests. For these reasons, it is important for teachers to create the most comfortable conditions possible for the assessment. Consider at least the lighting, the seating, and the testing materials and make any necessary adjustments *before* the test is administered.

- Provide stress relief. Many students with autism (and a number of students without the label too) experience anxiety about formal assessments. Some feel inadequate or unprepared to deal with the content or task being assessed. Others worry about how the results may be used, particularly in situations where a student's performance may result in a change in placement or teacher. In still other cases, the individual may not trust the process of assessment or the person administering the assessment (especially if that individual is a stranger). To minimize all these concerns, give the student some say in how, when, or with whom she will be assessed. Or give the individual choices in test format, design, or materials.

- Be flexible. Many formal assessments require students to give a single correct answer, allowing for little flexibility in interpretation. This can be frustrating for students who don't quite understand the directions or those who struggle mightily with the physical act of writing or those who can't easily translate their ideas onto paper. One way to address this challenge is to allow the student to select a few items from the test that he would rather explain orally than write.

- Provide *very* clear directions. For example, a student might interpret the "best" answer as the most humorous one or the one that she simply liked best, as opposed to the correct answer. Provide brief but very clear directions. If you are not the one writing the test and you are able only to adapt the instrument, it can be just as effective to take a fluorescent pen and highlight just the key words in each set of directions. Other ways to make directions more clear are to read the test directions to the learner or have the student repeat directions to you or to a peer to insure comprehension.

- Keep it predictable. Bear in mind that most of your students will perform better on assessments when they have experience with both the process and instruments being used. When your students are seeing or using a method or assessment for the first time, you can prepare them in a number of different ways. For example, you might give a practice test that contains the same types of items students will see on the real test. You can also ease tension and increase performance by simply giving student information about the content, format, setting, and time the assessment will take place.

- Adapt tests. Of all the assessments teachers use, tests probably produce the most anxiety for students. For this reason, you might want to create a few testing adaptations. For instance, you could allow them to answer one question with a partner; change the format of the test (from, say, filling in the blank to multiple choice), add extra credit, let them skip an item, allow retakes, give two tests and allow students to use their best score; have the student construct several or all test items, or weight some items more heavily (depending on the student's needs and strengths).

- Employ a range of strategies and tools. Some students with autism struggle with any type of test or formal assessment, but will be able to tell or show you what they have learned within the context of daily work. For this reason it is best to use a wide range of assessment tools, instruments, and methods to get the best sense of what the learner knows and can do. Observations, interviews, work samples, learning logs, anecdotal records, checklists, projects, demonstrations, portfolios, journals, exhibitions, student-created tests, presentations, formal papers, essays, reflections, collaborative quizzes, games, art, and focus groups are all examples of assessments that will help teachers gather a wide range of information about learner needs and abilities. Using a variety of assessments may be especially crucial when teaching students with autism because difficulties with reading, writing, or communicating can prevent a student from adequately completing a traditional assessment (such as a worksheet or a quiz) and may lead a teacher to believe that a student is less knowledgeable or capable than he actually is. For instance, a student who is unable to draw five circles may instead be able to pick five blocks out of a bucket. A student who cannot read aloud may in fact be a reader, but you might have to interview his mother to find out how he demonstrates that skill.

- Remember that just because you can't see it, that doesn't mean it isn't there! You need to consider what assessment will look like for students with more moderate and significant disabilities. Because these students have a hard time showing and communicating what they know and can do, teachers will need to be very creative with their assessment approaches. If a student cannot use traditional assessment tools, you may need to rely on methods such as observation, work samples, and interviews with parents or other staff members. Find out how the child demonstrates learning. Look for evidence of growth, and try to document it in a variety of ways. Videotape and audiotape may be particularly helpful in capturing evidence of learning and performance over time. Finally, be sure to assess the child across environments and using different materials so you can be sure to provide every opportunity for that student to show what she knows and can do.

3.17. Supports and Strategies for Literacy Lessons

Too many students with autism receive inadequate literacy instruction, and some receive none at all. All students—regardless of label, disability, communication needs, or perceived cognitive abilities—need literacy instruction to be productive, lead enjoyable lives, and, of course, to succeed in school. The supports and strategies that follow should help your students on the spectrum improve their reading and writing skills.

Reading

- Read. When a teacher reads aloud, learners learn new vocabulary words, get to hear what a fluent reader does (such as reading with expression or pausing at the end of sentences) and gain access to books and other materials they could not approach independently. For this reason (and many others), every teacher should read aloud to students every day. For teachers of young children, this is the norm, but as students advance to upper elementary levels, this practice becomes less common. This practice is also not common enough in the educational experiences of students with significant disabilities.

- Press play. Introduce books on tape or read-aloud books on the computer for students who cannot (or appear to be unable to) read on their own.

- Adapt books so that your students can access them. Enlarge text, rewrite the book or sections of it to make the text less complex, highlight key or familiar words, add icons or illustrations, or scan them into a PowerPoint presentation so that your student can turn pages with a switch or a mouse.

- Introduce a range of reading materials including magazines, newspapers, fiction and nonfiction books, comics, newsletters, and pamphlets. Remember to include items that may be of particular interest to the learner on the spectrum. Students with autism and Asperger labels have been known to enjoy reading phone books, catalogs, transportation schedules, almanacs, advertisements, contracts and other legal documents, appliance manuals, and the liner notes on CDs, and DVD cases, to name a few. Any of these can be included in your literacy curriculum.

- Provide a text-rich environment and text-rich materials, even when you are not sure whether a given student is a reader. Put labels on picture schedules and on augmentative communication devices. Also label objects in the classroom such as "chalkboard" and "stapler," but don't stop there. No matter what the perceived abilities of the students, add more sophisticated vocabulary as well, such as "aquarium," "credenza," and "sill." It certainly won't hurt, and students may just surprise you with their ability to learn new words.

- Capitalize on unique interests. If a student loves helicopters, the teacher can find literature, nonfiction texts, and even training manuals about helicopters. She can find other words that can be spelled with the letters of the word *helicopter*, write stories from the vantage point of different types of helicopters (such as a weather chopper or Blackhawk), and learn vocabulary related to aviation and transportation.

- To help students read more fluently, use echo reading (the teacher reads and then the student reads) or choral reading strategies (teacher and students read together).

- Give opportunities for repeated readings of the same text. These readings allow learners to feel successful, gain confidence, and read more independently. Fun ways to engineer repeated readings include reviewing favorite poems, having older students read a favorite book to several younger students, or having learners perform and practice a play, skit, or Reader's Theater.

- Pay attention to comprehension. If the student doesn't seem to understand what she reads, act out all or parts of the story or text with her. Or stop reading with the student at different intervals and talk about what is happening in the story. Or stop reading at different intervals and have the student draw what is happening in the story. You can also help boost comprehension by previewing what will be read and giving the student a specific purpose for reading: "We are going to learn about something very embarrassing that happens to Maggie at the dance. Can you guess what it is? Let's read and find out." You can even have the student write the purpose on a sticky note and keep it on her desk. Remember also that some students do comprehend what they read (or hear), but cannot effectively communicate their understanding, so be sure to assess comprehension in a variety of ways.

Writing

- Introduce a wide range of writing materials, including colored pencils, paint pens, drawing and painting software programs, "sensory" art supplies (shaving cream and pudding), markers, stickers, charcoal, tools for printmaking (potatoes or blocks), computers (word-processing programs), communication devices, typewriters, rubber stamps (pictures, letters, or words), magnetic letters or words, and letter guides. Keep interests in mind as you gather writing tools.

- Make writing part of the daily routine. Give students meaningful opportunities across the school day to write for enjoyment, for different audiences, and for authentic reasons. This recommendation may be even more critical for students with disabilities who need practice not only with writing but with communication in general. To motivate students to write often and improve their skills, provide plenty of brief opportunities to write every day. For instance, assign a "one thing I learned today" reflection during the last five minutes of class, dialogue to students in their journals, or have students write morning greetings to each other. Even if these are cloze activities or require only a sentence, writing informally as part of the routine can help students improve their fluency and understand writing as fun and purposeful. These activities are appropriate for those who can write independently, as well as for those using augmentative and alternative communication. A student who is just learning to use a multilevel device, for instance, can work with a teacher to construct a "miniletter" of one or two phrases or sentences. A student who is working with a picture communication system can combine images to create sentences and send notes to peers.

- Have students write stories about their own lives and experiences. Some students may need to use a lot of pictures to tell stories. You might let these learners use a digital camera to not only record their environment or capture life in the classroom but also to create and document stories they invent. For example, you could encourage a student or group of students to create a story about a classroom bully. After they draft the story events, students can act out scenes from the narrative as the teacher or another student takes photos of the scenes. The story can be assembled, and individual students can add their own dialogue and details to each photo.

- Use what is already there. To get students into writing, use the materials they already like. For instance, provide the student a copy of his favorite picture book without the text. Then have the student write the book in his own words. If he doesn't want to veer from the original language or plot line, allow him to create a sequel. If your student prefers fiction to nonfiction, the same strategy can be used or you can use informational text as an inspiration for stories and poems. One teacher we know had her student write "An Ode to an Oldsmobile" using information from an old car dealer brochure he kept in his backpack.

- Pay attention. If you hear a student act out scenes from favorite movies, copy the monologue or dialogue onto paper and use it as a story starter. If the person enjoys making a list of favorite zoo animals, use the list as the framework for a poem.

- Encourage students to use technology (such as Web site design, new computer programs, or instant messaging) to increase literacy skills. Reluctant writers might be motivated by voice-activated software or by using an old typewriter instead of a paper and pen. Struggling readers may be more likely to engage in phonemic awareness activities when you offer computer games instead of worksheets.

- Change the format or product. A student who does not produce much with a notebook or computer might be interested in writing dialogue if she can fill in the speech bubbles of comic book characters.

- Move beyond presence to participation. Look for ways for students with significant disabilities to participate in writing instruction and lessons. For instance, a child using a communication device can choose the characters and setting for a story while a peer chooses the plot. As they construct a story together, the peer can stop periodically and ask for input—such as "Do you think we should have him fall off the ladder or fall off the roof?" A speech therapist or teacher can work with students to be sure the necessary vocabulary is in place or it can be quickly created.

3.18. Supports and Strategies for Math Lessons

While some students on the spectrum have special talents in math, many also struggle to learn math skills and competencies and will need a host of supports and strategies to succeed. Following are some ideas to implement in your math lessons:

- Use plenty of manipulatives and a variety of materials to teach math concepts. Dominoes, real money, Unifex cubes, fraction bars, counting animals, play clocks, timers, food, scales, games, rulers, dice, marbles, and abacai are all examples of items that K–12 teachers can employ. If a learner finds it too challenging to work with the materials while learning new content, the teacher can use the materials at the front of the room and give the student time to work with the items at a later time.

- Encourage the use of calculators (or even adding machines for those who like gadgets and the accompanying sounds and motions). Make sure the keys are large enough for the learner to use easily.

- Computers play a significant role in the learning of many students on the spectrum. Programs that allow students to learn at their own pace can be of particular help in inclusive classrooms where teachers are seeking ways to personalize instruction without having students work in self-contained settings. As with all computer programs, use care when choosing them. Those that have too many "bells and whistles," colors, and noises may be annoying or even distressing to students on the spectrum.

- Allow for some mental math. Math teachers often demand that students "show their work." This can be a challenge for some students on the spectrum who can do computations in their heads but have a hard time explaining (or in some cases even knowing) how they got to the answer. You may need to make accommodations for these learners. You might, for example, request that the student show you his work for only a few of the problems, or you could have him talk you through the process instead of having him write out the steps.

- Be aware of story-problem pitfalls. Students with autism may struggle to solve problems that are set in a social context. For instance, some (though not all) students on the spectrum may find the following problem hard or even impossible to solve, even if they can easily calculate $3 - 1 = 2$: "Sari has three apples. She sees that Jon doesn't have any apples. She can see that Jon is hungry, so she decides to give him one of her apples. How many apples does Sari have now?" Some students will find the extra language hard to process; others will be frustrated trying to figure out the social interaction between Sally and Jon. This consideration does not mean students should be exempt from story problems, but the teacher may want to note the fact that students who cannot do story problems may still know the answer to the calculation. In addition, a teacher may want to show a student how to use a highlighter to emphasize the specific pieces information needed to solve the equation or act out the problem with the student so she can better comprehend the problem and arrive at the answer more easily.

- For students needing extra help, consider creating a "math helper" notebook with tips and cues related to different math units. This book might include, among other tools, a multiplication table, a calendar, a number line, examples of different types of graphs, and an English-to-metric conversion table. With this type of support, students may be able to participate in more complex math lessons with peers, even if they have not yet mastered certain skills or memorized certain pieces of information.

- Show and tell when possible. Have students create a line graph by asking them to line up in rows. Make a pizza to teach fractions. Ask children to stand in small groups and then larger groups to teach sets and subsets. Take students on a field trip to find geometric shapes in architecture.

- Explicitly teach the language of mathematics to students with autism. For instance, a child with autism who struggles with language may not understand that *add, combine*, and *put together* all mean the same thing. A list of these terms hanging in the classroom or stuck inside the learner's math book will be a useful tool.

- Practice math skills across situations and environments. Help the student calculate lunch money, buy a soda at the school store, or count how many snacks are needed for the class party.

3.19. Helping Students Manage Homework

Many parents deal with daily homework difficulties. Parents of students on the spectrum are no different and may face additional challenges. Students on the spectrum, for example, may need more downtime at home than other students. They may also have great difficulty explaining the assignments to their parents because of language problems or communication differences. Following are some ways to help your students on the spectrum deal with these difficulties and others:

- Assign work that the students can do on their own or with minimal support from parents. This may mean that you have to adapt the assignments for some students on the spectrum.

- Assign it again. Give the same format or quantity of homework repeatedly, if possible (such as practicing twenty vocabulary words, playing a computer learning game, reading ten pages from a chapter book, finishing one workbook page, or reviewing flashcards), so the learner does not have to remember and learn new directions over and over again and so parents also know what is expected night after night.

- Consider assigning homework at the beginning of class. Students are more likely to be alert and attentive at that point and, in the case of students on the spectrum, less likely to be focusing on the upcoming transition.

- Help the student to record her homework in an assignment notebook or, for students who are more motivated by technology, in her phone or PDA. Set aside a few moments each day for her to just record assignments and gather necessary materials.

- Relate homework to students' lives, their interests, and their strengths whenever possible. If a student loves James Bond, for instance, send his work home in a briefcase. If the student has a dog he adores, encourage him to study with his pet.

- Allow alternative formats for assignments, such as giving students a choice of a photo or written essay or letting students send their homework via e-mail to eliminate the risk of losing assignments.

- Make it shorter. Cutting out some problems, steps, or assignments will be necessary for students who cannot sit for long periods or for those who require a lot of downtime once they get home.

- Break big assignments into small steps. If your sixth graders need to write a two-page report on China, for example, the student on the spectrum may need the project broken down. You might create a list like this:

  1. Review three different resources used in class
  2. Write down at least three topics you want to address in your report
  3. Write a paragraph on each of these three topics
  4. Add an introduction, transitions, and a conclusion
  5. Have the teacher, a parent, or a friend read your rough draft
  6. Read their feedback
  7. Make any needed changes
  8. Type a clean copy

  You might also want to provide an example of another report so that the learner can see what the expectations are.

- Adapt the goals or standards for the homework of the student on the spectrum. For instance, you may decide to give points for getting homework in on time and following directions, as well as for correct answers. You can also set alternative goals for student performance. For instance, you could tell the student she doesn't necessarily have to complete homework every night, but she must work on it for at least twenty minutes.

- Let them keep track. A method that some teachers find helpful (and one that some learners on the spectrum find very compelling) is charting or graphing homework completion. Having students place a sticker or mark on a calendar for each day the work is submitted on time can be motivating. This is especially true for students who like to tally, add, average, or otherwise keep tabs!

- Not everyone can do everything, but everyone can do something. Remember: even students with more moderate and significant disabilities can be assigned homework if it is appropriate. Just remember to keep it manageable. Younger students might be asked to spend time looking at picture books or finding objects related to an upcoming lesson (such as things that are round or things that begin with the letter G). Older students might be asked to interview their parent about a given topic or find pictures in magazines related to grade-level content.

3.20. Making Within-School Transitions Easier for Students

For some students with autism and Asperger syndrome, moving from classroom to classroom and activity to activity can be stressful. Following are some ways to make within-school transitions easier for your students on the spectrum:

- Follow a routine as much as possible, so that transitions become more predictable. In addition, make sure all staff members handle transitions in the same ways.

- Be aware of unplanned transitions. Keep in mind all the transitions that may occur in a day, a week, a month, or a year that cannot always be predicted. Tornado drills, impromptu assemblies, seating changes in classrooms, power outages, early dismissal due to weather, other students leaving school due to illness, and substitute teachers are just a few examples of these additional transitions. In these cases, you might designate an "emergency transition" person to check in with and help the person on the spectrum as needed. You might also have some supports in place that you can draw on when difficulties arise as a result of unanticipated transitions (such as a book about dealing with changes).

- Let them know when it is almost time to go. Give five-minute and one-minute reminders to the whole class before difficult transitions.

- Do something. Provide the student or entire class with a transitional activity such as writing in a homework notebook or, for younger students, singing a song about cleaning up.

- Ask peers to help. In elementary classrooms, teachers can ask all students to move from place to place with a partner. In middle and high school classrooms, students with autism might choose a peer to walk with during passing time.

- Provide a transition aid. Some students need to carry a toy, object, picture, or other aid to facilitate their movement from one place to the next. One student we know carries a rabbit's foot from class to class. He leaves it at the door and picks it up again when he needs to move to a new room. Some students need an object that helps them focus specifically on the next environment or activity. A student might, for instance, carry a tennis ball on his way to the playground or a paintbrush on his way to art class.

- Offer advance warning before abrupt or challenging transitions when you can. If you know there will be an earthquake drill during the day, ask for permission from the principal to inform the student privately of the event.

- Sign out with students. If you are going to be out of the classroom for a scheduled meeting or other absence and a substitute teacher will be taking your place, make sure to tell your student and, if needed, write it into her schedule.

3.21. Making School-to-School Transitions Easier for Students

When a family moves or when it is simply time for a student to move from one building to another, the transition to new teachers and a new environment can be overwhelming for the learner on the spectrum. By using some of these ideas, however, teachers can make the process easier and less disruptive:

- Provide a student-at-a-glance sheet for the new teachers or team.

- Give a preview of the school. Students with autism will profit from seeing, experiencing, and learning about the school before they show up on the first day.

- Have siblings, parents, or friends describe the new school.

- Provide brochures and photographs of the school. A yearbook will also be helpful for some learners.

- Give a virtual tour. Visit the school's Web site and learn about the various programs, classes, and spaces.

- Provide newsletters from the previous year. Read the articles with or to the student. Talk about the events and people featured and show him the accompanying photographs. This can be a helpful exercise for any student, even those who cannot ask questions or read the materials on their own.

- Facilitate an interview. Have students construct questions about the school or new classes, and ask teachers to answer those questions in writing or on audiotape.

- Put your filmmaking skills to work. Some learners might appreciate a videotape of the school and its rooms, complete with short interviews with their new teachers (such as "Hi, I'm Ms. Merced, and I'm going to be your fifth-grade teacher. In this room we work hard, but we have a lot of fun too"). You can also videotape the student in the new school engaging in favorite activities such as shooting hoops in the gym or playing piano in the music room.

- Collaborate to ease the transition. In some cases it may be possible for the teacher or a team from the new school to arrange to come to the old school for a short visit to meet with and observe the student and his previous team. This can give the new team valuable information and help stimulate ideas for supports needed in the new setting.

- Invite new teachers to observe the student in the "old" school to give them a sense of how he fares in a comfortable environment. If teachers cannot visit, send a videotaped diary of his school day including images of the student engaged in favorite activities and scenes that include some of the key adaptations that are used to support the person (such as special seating, math manipulatives, a personal schedule, assistive technology, or an augmentative communication device).

3.22. Preventing Behavior Struggles in the Classroom

Many of the difficulties faced in school by students on the spectrum can be prevented. Meeting sensory, communication, and social needs is well over half the battle when it comes to preventing difficult moments. Following are some specific suggestions for meeting those needs and preventing behavior struggles for your students on the spectrum:

- Watch your language. Evaluate how you talk and think about the student, even when you are away from him. Do you see students as "hyper" or "active," as "behavior problems" or "students with behavior struggles," or "being obsessed" or "having fascinations"? Language can drive practice, help us see students differently, and prompt us to provide more sensitive supports.

- All students respond well to high expectations. Strive to look for competence in students and see the best in them.

- Address only those behaviors that affect the student's ability to learn, classroom safety, or health. Behaviors that are seen as odd or even interfering may actual serve the purpose of keeping the student calm. For example, a student may hum softly to himself or flick his fingers in front of eyes to relax or decompress.

- Try to meet student needs. It is important to remember that many behavior struggles are a result of sensory, communication, or physical difficulties. Set the student up for success by creating a comfortable classroom environment, taking her learning style into account when planning lessons, and providing opportunities and supports for clear communication.

- Look for sensory offenders. Challenging behavior can be triggered by hypersensitivity to certain sensory stimuli.

Sometimes those without autism do not consciously notice these stimuli, such as a flickering light or a sound in the distance. Do a quick assessment of the environment to see if there are obvious sensory "violations" in the space. For instance, you may want to turn the overhead lights off or ask students to stop using the pencil sharpener.

- Provide plenty of opportunities for movement throughout the day. Build walking or sensory breaks into the day for the purpose of regulating and releasing tension. When an individual seems especially frustrated or out of sorts, look for opportunities for vigorous exercise (such as running laps with a friend or staying after school for a swim).

- Offer a "safe space." This space should not be viewed as a punishment, but as a retreat that can be used to avoid difficulties. A safe space might be outside the classroom, in a stairwell, the nurse's office, a corner of the library, or even a nook in the classroom itself.

- Teach by the numbers. Help the student recognize and interpret feelings that lead to difficult moments. Use a number scale or similar tool to enable the student to describe and visualize his emotional state. Then teach about different scenarios. For example, if a student loses the cap to his pen he might put himself at 2 out of 10 on the scale. If it rains on the day of his tennis tournament, that might rate 6 out of 10. If he is physically hurt, that might rate a 9 or a 10. Teaching and discussing this process during calm moments makes it more likely the student will be able to draw on the language and descriptions when he is feeling stressed.

- Be explicit about rules, norms, and procedures. Negative or interfering behaviors can occur when students are confused or unaware of expectations. Provide a list of school and classroom rules in a student's notebook or desk as well as a list of ideas that she can use to deal with challenges.

- Check the curriculum. Make sure the child's day is appropriately motivating, and challenging. If the person is often alone and does not experience novelty, interaction, and joy in the day, he or she will likely find it challenging to "behave."

- Think beyond smiles and frowns. Avoid categorizing each hour or segment of the day as either good or bad—such as "How did you do in math?" or "Were you good during first period?" Many behavior programs put students in a position of being evaluated and assessed day in and out (such as a smiley face for a segment of good behavior and a frown for a segment of bad behavior). Such constant scrutiny can be very stressful and is not the best way to set students up for success.

- Talk on paper. Even students with reliable communication may have difficulty asking for help or explaining why they are upset. At these times it can be helpful to ask the student to have a conversation with you on paper or on e-mail or even via text messaging. The indirect nature of this kind of exchange can help some learners communicate more effectively.

For more information on behavior issues, see Checklist 4.17: Addressing Challenging Behavior and Checklist 4.18: Strategies for Coping in Crisis, both in Section Four.

3.23. Don'ts for Working with Students with Autism

In general, we embrace an "over, under, around, or through" philosophy to educating students. In other words, we believe teachers should try a range of ideas, try again, and keep trying until they find success. There are a few strategies, however, that we discourage using with students with autism, and these should not be part of any teacher's approach even as they "try, try, and try again." Here is our short list of habits and methods and thoughts to avoid:

- Don't assume that you understand the needs of *all* students with autism after you have taught one student on the spectrum (or read a book on autism or watched a documentary on it). If you know *one* student with autism, you know only one student with autism. Although students do share some characteristics in common, they are more diverse than they are similar.

- Don't assume that a student who is exhibiting challenging behavior *intends* to be difficult. Students on the spectrum may engage in any number of behaviors because of struggles with communication, social skills, or even their sensory system.

- Don't get locked into arguments with students. You won't "win," and the student can become more confused because of the increased use of language and the escalation of the situation in general.

- Don't use favorite objects and fascinations only as rewards. Infuse these things into daily activities, lessons, and materials to motivate, interest, and inspire students. And when it comes to students' most prized objects or activities (those needed for comfort and daily support), don't use them for rewards at all.

- Don't insist on eye contact. Respect gaze avoidance, and realize students are often more successful at attending to the teacher or the lesson when they look away or use their peripheral vision.

- Don't punish or reprimand a student for behaviors that result from her autism, such as flapping her arms, failing to move or respond to a request quickly, avoiding eye contact, being disorganized, having an outburst during a difficult transition, or misunderstanding verbal directions.

- Don't be afraid to ask the student for help in solving a problem or brainstorming solutions. Students with reliable communication may be able to help you figure out a good adaptation for the classroom or a good behavior support for themselves.

- Don't hesitate to partner with families to design a better educational program, address behavior struggles, or develop new teaching strategies. You can do these things informally by asking questions and opening a dialogue or formally by observing successful family activities or brainstorming solutions to a specific problem with parents or even siblings.

3.24. Helping Students with Autism Shine

Perhaps the most important list in the book, this set of suggestions is meant to help teachers focus on what learners *can* do and highlight gifts and abilities that are too often hidden or unrecognized. It is also intended to foster empowerment. Following are some ways to help your students on the spectrum shine:

- Store successes. Keep a folder or small box of the student's best work so he can look at these products to gain confidence or get a boost on a difficult day.

- Give students as much information as you can about their abilities. Talk specifically about what they do well. For example, "You are very honest and have a real sense of justice" is more specific and helpful than "You are a good citizen."

- Let the student know about his strengths, his growth, and his gifts in a variety of different ways. Call home when the student has done something particularly well (such as helped a peer or mastered a new skill). Praise him on his poetry and suggest that he submit something to the school literary journal.

- Capitalize on areas of expertise. Many students have passions or fascinations they love to share with others. Encourage these students to tutor or teach others about these topics. Better yet, create a group or club around the fascination, if appropriate, so the individual can take a valued leadership role.

- Let them give instead of receive. A lot of students with autism get support from others, including other students. Engineer opportunities, whenever possible, for these learners to *give* support. Students with milder disabilities can tutor others or provide a service to others. Students with more moderate and significant disabilities can give support as well. A student who is nonverbal can listen while others practice reading or he can perform simple jobs around the classroom.

- Include. Be sure to include students with autism labels in every schoolwide program designed to recognize achievements, reward good citizenship, or celebrate contributions (such as student of the week and good citizenship award programs).

- Build on "what works." Don't reinvent the wheel! Talk to teachers and other staff members about what the student does well and what strategies are effective. For a planning tool you can use to collect this information, go to Paula's website and download the strengths and strategies worksheet (www.paulakluth.com/articles/stregthsstrateg.html). This tool will help teams consider all of the learner's gifts, skills, and abilities as they plan strategies for support.

4

MORE HELPFUL STRATEGIES FOR HOME AND SCHOOL

Introduction

How can I be a better communication partner for a person on the spectrum? What do I do when a person with autism is in crisis? Are there ways I can help somebody with auditory sensitivity? Questions like these are relevant for many different stakeholders, including self-advocates, families, teachers, paraprofessionals, therapists, social workers, counselors, psychologists, physicians, and community workers. This section contains lists that will be of interest to just about anybody who loves, cares for, supports, treats, or educates an individual on the spectrum.

We have included, for instance, checklists featuring issues that are key for different stages of life, including one on toddlers and preschoolers, one on young children, and one on adolescents. Many concerns and issues continue across the life span for people on the spectrum, including sensory problems, the need for advocacy, and related medical conditions. Other issues, however, morph and change from year to year. To that end, these three lists, though general, show you what to expect at different ages, which supports might be needed, and what unique issues need to be addressed. This section also features a short list of individuals who might be members of an evaluation or referral team, multidisciplinary team, or transition team. Of course, as the three stage-of-life lists suggest, the type of team you have will change as the years pass. This list, however, will give you an idea of the types of individuals you can expect to see at meetings and hear about as you plan for and learn from the person on the spectrum.

In this section, we also feature several lists that relate to the primary areas of challenge for those with autism and Asperger syndrome: communication, social skills, and movement issues. You will also find tips for dealing with sensory challenges. So many with autism and Asperger syndrome struggle with sounds, sights, and smells across different environments. They may also have difficulty with materials, textures, and touch in general. For these reasons, we have created lists that offer solutions for visual, tactile, auditory, and olfactory problems. Most of the ideas apply across environments and can be applied to classrooms, homes, and even some community settings.

Other lists provide suggestions for helping those on the spectrum learn, be productive, cope, and thrive. We have included one list on teaching and learning (across activities and environments), one on promoting organization, and one on helping individuals deal with change. These tips can all be shared with any stakeholder but may be of particular interest to the person on the spectrum him- or herself.

Two different lists on addressing challenges with behavior round out this section. We compiled one list to help readers prevent challenging behaviors and address needs as they arise. A second list is specifically designed for dealing with crisis situations; these ideas, we hope, will promote the use of sensitive and respectful supports and help the individual with autism.

In general, our aim for the ideas in this section is to help individuals on the spectrum live in greater comfort, safety, security, and independence. Although we have designed these lists to appeal to a broad audience, we hope we have provided ideas that those on the spectrum themselves would deem respectful and useful. And no matter who you are, remember that though none of these lists will provide every answer, we do hope that our thoughts can serve as a starting point for designing your own collection of effective tips, supports, and resources.

4.1. To Keep in Mind for Toddlers and Preschoolers

There are many special considerations for teaching and caring for little ones on the spectrum. Families will be dealing with a new diagnosis and negotiating a maze of services and supports. Educators, for their part, are not only looking for ways to help the student with autism but are often trying to aid families too. Following are some things to keep in mind when supporting toddlers and preschoolers on the spectrum:

- Join in. To build communication and social skills, look for opportunities to involve the child in preschool programs and activities such as "Mommy and Me" music or movement classes, play dates, story time at the library, and park district play groups.

- Make repeat trips to favorite spots. Going to the same park over and over again increases the chances that you will run into the same families and children over time and thereby build relationships with them.

- Get on the floor and in the tree house. Young children may need help figuring out how to play and communicate with someone who acts, talks, or behaves differently than they do. For this reason, you may need to "play along" when the child on the spectrum interacts with a new child and show the pair or the group how to interact, communicate, take turns, and have fun together.

- To make social interactions more predictable, invite other families and children to your home to play. Encourage activities that don't necessarily require children to share treasured toys or learn complicated rules. Coloring a mural, decorating cupcakes, dancing to silly songs, running in the sprinkler, playing on a jungle gym, building with blocks, and blowing bubbles are all good examples of play that is noncompetitive and lots of fun.

- Use plenty of visual supports both at home and in the community. A picture checklist can be created to plan out a day at the zoo, for instance. A small book with pictures of grandma and grandpa can be given to the child as the family drives across town for a visit.

- Use music to inspire, teach, and motivate. Small children will often learn new behaviors more quickly if these are paired with motivating music. Create or use little songs or rhymes for routines such as cleaning up toys, washing hands, going to bed, or getting in the car.

- Use rituals and routines to help the child feel safe and be successful. For example, use a predictable bedtime routine, end therapy sessions with the same game each week, and set up a step-by-step procedure for setting the table or getting ready for the bath.

- Incorporate children's literature and movies to teach skills and provide information. Young children may respond better to a safety video than to a minilecture from mom and dad on the topic. Polite behavior can be taught by collecting and sharing books about good manners, especially books that feature favorite characters or objects.

4.2. To Keep in Mind for School-Age Children

Starting school means a new learning environment, new community experiences (such as clubs, sports, and birthday parties), and possibly even changes in family life as students spend more time away from home. Following are some considerations for supporting school-age children on the spectrum:

- The support team grows in the elementary years. As students begin kindergarten, an array of individuals can become involved in planning and supporting the child with autism: more than one teacher, several therapists, a school psychologist, a social worker, and possibly even a separate case manager. At this point it becomes more important to keep careful records, know who does what, and take notes at meetings.

- School-age children have to go through a lot of transitions that they did not have in preschool or daycare. Even as early as first grade, students may need to travel from classroom to classroom for some instruction, move to the playground and back to the classroom more than once, and traverse the hallways for special subject classes such as art, music, gym, or computer class. Supports will be needed for those who feel overwhelmed by so many changes and so much movement. A transition object, mantra, or ritual may be necessary. (See Checklist 3.20: Making Within-School Transitions Easier for Students for more on transitions.)

- Skills related to making friends, cooperating with others, and meeting new people are key for school-age children. These skills should be taught in the context of the curriculum via community-building activities, cooperative learning, and even by introducing literature with these themes. Skills can also be taught explicitly through videos, modeling, and social skill instruction. (See Checklist 4.8: Strategies for Building Social Skills in this section for more ideas.)

- Self-advocacy begins around this time. When children have become old enough to go to school, it is the perfect time to start inviting them to their own individualized education plan (IEP) meetings. Very small children might attend for just a few minutes to pass out some of their work samples or to present photos of the past year's successes. Children older than ten or eleven can stay and contribute to the meeting in a more formal way.

- To encourage friendships and help build communication and social skills, look for opportunities to involve the child in extracurricular activities, groups, and teams. To be sure that the individual enjoys the experience, research a wide range of activities, including park and recreation opportunities, school and extracurricular options, and other community offerings. Not every child will be excited about joining a baseball team. Some will be more interested in individual sports such as swimming or academic options such as Web site design or math club.

- As students grow up, they will begin spending more time away from home and family and more time with other adults. Be sure that everyone involved in the child's life knows emergency information, has the parents' phone numbers, and understands procedures for behavior challenges or medical problems. You may also want to devise a system of communication for getting and giving information to various team members.

4.3. To Keep in Mind for Adolescents and Teenagers

For most individuals, adolescence and the teen years are a mixture of excitement and difficulty. Students in middle school and high school may enjoy taking new risks, having new experiences, and becoming more independent. At the same time, they may be less than thrilled about dealing with social challenges, physical and emotional changes, and, of course, changes in services as they transition from school to life in the community. Following are some considerations for supporting adolescents and teens on the spectrum:

- Adolescence is the perfect time for individuals on the spectrum to learn self-advocacy and behaviors associated with advocacy. Some students begin by educating their peers about autism or even writing books or designing Web sites about their experiences. Teachers and parents can use advocacy as a tool for widening the individual's social circle, teaching new skills (such as public speaking or using a communication device), and even for honing literacy skills such as writing, editing, and reading across genres. Teens who initially do not seem interested in self-advocacy may become interested if they read autobiographies of people with autism, attend autism conferences, or meet other teens who are advocates. All of these are activities that can be introduced by parents or school staff.

- Peers will undoubtedly begin to play a bigger role in the child's life at this stage. Since all forms of autism have an impact on social development, most adolescents on the spectrum will have social challenges. They may appear indifferent when peers try to interact or, conversely, they may be very sensitive to the behaviors and responses of peers. Give support around these issues by being open, giving advice when it is solicited, providing help through literature, and even seeking help from support groups or peer mentors (perhaps even others on the spectrum) if needed.

- As individuals with autism grow older and sexuality becomes more of an issue at home and at school, a variety of topics will need to be addressed. Some of these topics include intimate relationships, sex education (including sexual abuse education), self-care, and hygiene. In some cases, significant sexuality-related challenges arise such as stripping or masturbating in public, touching others, and talking about inappropriate subject matter. The most important way to address all these needs is to talk about sexuality issues early and regularly (in other words, you will want to have had "the talk" long before questions or challenges arise); give youngsters a lot of information (not just warnings or severe words about "inappropriate behavior") and seek guidance from others, including school counselors, psychologists, social workers, or health professionals.

- Adolescence is a time when those on the spectrum, like all teens, will be more prone to mood swings and even depression. Possible signs are expression of more sadness than usual, expression of more anger or hostility than usual, more frequent crying or increased tearfulness, changes in eating and sleeping habits, and changes in interests (be especially watchful for a drop in interest in special fascinations).

- Age-appropriateness should be a concern as students age. When an individual is playing with toys meant for younger children, focusing on interests that are not relevant to his peer group, or engaging in activities that don't interest others his age, he may limit his opportunities for social relationships as well as miss out on experiences and activities that are geared more to his chronological age. Being concerned about age-appropriateness means paying attention to these experiences and activities in the person's life. It does not mean, however, taking favorite materials or activities away from somebody simply because they are deemed more suitable for someone younger. Attending to age appropriateness might involve making attempts to channel old interests into new ones. For example, if a young man loves a child's cartoon, we don't have to prevent him from enjoying it; we could instead try to expand his passion for the program into one that includes animation, cartooning, comic books, and animated films geared for older audiences (such as *The Simpsons* and Japanese anime).

- The search for part-time or full-time work may begin in adolescence. Parents and teachers can be helpful in this process by being open to conversations about various jobs, vocations, or careers and by avoiding harsh judgments about interests and choices. If an individual talks incessantly about becoming a race car driver, it is probably more helpful to say, "Race car driving does seem like a dream job," as opposed to "That job is not really appropriate for you." Then explore possibilities related to racing. Tour a local track, visit racing Web sites, and talk to a mechanic of specialty cars. These activities may help the person broaden her search and potentially find a rewarding job. You can also help by engaging in activities that will help the individual learn more about various occupations, such as reading books and magazine articles, browsing Web sites, taking field trips in the community, and attending job fairs and career days at local colleges.

- College and technical school may also be goals for the adolescent on the spectrum. Start talking early (in the early teen years) about these goals and explore options by visiting various Web sites, sending away for catalogs, and bringing him for campus visits. Students who have very specific goals in mind—such as attending a certain college or getting a particular degree—will need to do more long-range planning. If a youngster has his heart set on becoming a veterinary technician, for instance, you will want to help him get in touch with one or more individuals who have that job so he can ask questions and learn more about the work, set up a visit to a clinic or animal hospital to observe the job, identify the classes he needs now and in the near future, and map out the experiences he should have in the upcoming months and years. Parents should also be aware that several colleges and universities have started postsecondary education programs for students with moderate and significant disabilities. Although programs vary, in most of them students attend some classes, participate in extracurricular activities, and enjoy life on campus in general.

- In the preteen and teen years, there is more unstructured and unsupervised time outside of school for most individuals. This can be a chance to explore new ways to spend free time inside the home and outside the home. Listening to books on tape or to music, crafting, gardening, tackling home projects, surfing the Web, exercising, playing games, writing, reading, hobbies, and creating artwork are all relaxing ways to spend time at home. Joining clubs, visiting the library, taking walks or running, going to the gym, shopping, taking night classes, attending sporting events, volunteering, working, and visiting museums, galleries, gardens, zoos, or historic sites are all interesting ways to spend free time outside the home.

- Services can change a lot when students move from middle school to high school. Even more drastic is the change in services that occurs after the individual turns twenty-one. For this reason, it is recommended that teachers and families do everything possible to encourage an individual's independence and sense of personal agency during the adolescent and teen years. The more a person is able to do on her own (no matter how minimal), the easier it will be to secure employment and live as independently as possible in future.

4.4. Possible Members of a Support Team

An individual's team will change from year to year depending on grade level, age, school district, and what types of needs are assessed. Following are just some of the members a person with autism may have on his team:

- *Person on the spectrum:* may function in any number of roles on the team. In many cases—such as when the person is planning a transition to work and community living—this person will be the team leader. In other cases, such as with young children, he will contribute ideas for his program by sharing favorite activities, topics, or materials.

- *Family members:* depending on the person and that individual's situation, this may be a mom or dad or mom *and* dad or any combination of parents, guardians, aunts, uncles, grandparents, and even siblings.

- *Social worker:* a professional trained to talk with people and their families about emotional or physical needs and find support services for them.

- *Child psychiatrist:* a medical doctor who may be involved in diagnosis and specializes in the behavior and emotional aspects of infants, children, and adolescents.

- *Clinical psychologist:* specializes in understanding the nature and impact of developmental disabilities, including autism; may perform psychological assessments.

- *Developmental pediatrician:* a physician who addresses the special needs or issues of children with disabilities.

- *Neurologist:* a medical doctor trained in the diagnosis and treatment of nervous system disorders, including diseases of the brain, spinal cord, nerves, and muscles.

- *General education teacher:* teacher of general curriculum who will collaborate with special educator and other team members if the individual on the spectrum receives services in a regular education classroom.

- *Special education teacher:* works with children with disabilities; most instruct students at the elementary, middle, and secondary school level, although some work with infants and toddlers.

- *Occupational therapist:* focuses on daily living skills such as eating, grooming, and dressing; occupational therapists also address sensory issues, fine motor skills, and coordination of movement.

- *Physical therapist:* a health professional who uses exercises and other methods to restore or maintain the body's strength, mobility, and function.

- *Speech or language therapist:* a professional involved in the improvement of communication skills by evaluating speech production, speech comprehension, and swallowing function.

- *Paraprofessional:* a trained worker who is not a member of the teaching profession but who assists the teaching staff with anything from providing instruction to supporting therapies to facilitating social relationships for the student on the spectrum.

4.5. Strategies for Encouraging and Facilitating Communication

Open any textbook on autism or disability, and you will find several pages and perhaps several chapters dedicated to improving the communication skills or capacities of students with autism. Less common, however, are pages and chapters dedicated to the necessary skills, attitudes, beliefs, and abilities of the communication partner. This paradigm or view of seeing communication improvement as a task for only one person in the dyad is puzzling, because communication is undoubtedly a social act. Therefore, supporting a student's communication will involve more than engaging in an assessment or encouraging his participation in a small-group discussion. Supporting communication also involves reflection, self-examination, and collaboration. Following are suggestions for becoming a better communication partners for students on the spectrum:

- Observe the individual to get information about his communication preferences. Does he communicate most effectively when he is in a quiet setting, when he is deeply engaged in a favorite video game, or when he is riding calmly in the car?

- Don't insist on eye contact—or, to put it another way, remember to respect gaze avoidance. When we want someone's attention, we typically expect eye contact. Many who know and love those with autism, however, understand that eye contact can be irritating or even painful for these students. We now know that many people cannot pay attention to a conversation when they are making eye contact with their communication partner. For many people, doing so can require too much scanning for and interpreting of nonverbal communication resulting in loss of the verbal message.

- Playing with voice volume, quality, and tone can be helpful in connecting with any student, including those with autism. If the person does not seem to be responding to you, switch to a softer voice. If the person does not follow a direction you have given, use a sing-song voice or try an accent of some kind instead.

- Whispering can also be a very effective way to capture the attention of a person who seems inattentive or distracted. It may be helpful to use when the individual does not seem to understand what you are saying or when the situation is chaotic or confusing.

- Use more than one mode of output, if needed. If there appears to be a communication breakdown, try writing your message as well as speaking it. E-mail or texting are good tools for this type of communication. Even if you are sitting right next to the person, try sitting down on two different computers and sending instant messages back and forth.

- Try using indirect communication if the person seems to struggle in the conversation. Many individuals find less direct means of communication more comfortable and less risky than face-to-face conversation and interaction. You can make dialogue less direct by simply writing or to the person instead of having a verbal exchange. People on the spectrum may also respond well to a communication partner who uses e-mail or the telephone (even if both of you are in the same room), speaks with an accent, uses a puppet, doll, or props (such as a toy microphone, a megaphone, or a secret decoder ring), sings, or uses rhythmic language.

- If you want an individual to learn new skills and gain communication competence, communication opportunities must be created for her. In the classroom, for instance, teachers can provide opportunities for learners to communicate and share regularly. Structures that can be used include "turn and talk," where the teacher pauses regularly to give students a chance to share something with a partner, or a "whip" structure (Harmin, 1995) where the teacher calls on students one by one to share a phrase related to the classroom content (such as naming one healthy food or sharing one way to be ecologically responsible). At home, families can create rituals that encourage communication in a structured way. For example, during dinner, each family member can share a "new" or a "good," meaning one good thing that happened today or one piece of news. A weekly phone call to grandma might be turned into an opportunity for the individual to provide a succinct summary of the week's activities. Story time can be a time to practice new sign language vocabulary or use a new device.

- Some individuals interpret language literally. They may need help interpreting figurative language like idioms, jokes, riddles, metaphors, slang, and sarcasm. Offering support for an individual with these difficulties might involve double-checking to make sure directions or questions are understood, providing opportunities for individuals to learn about language (by presenting a "metaphor of the week," for example), using visuals to help individuals learn or remember the meanings of figurative language (such as drawing a cartoon of a child with big ears and a picture of a water jug to show what is meant by the phrase, "little pitchers have big ears"), or encouraging the person to keep a personal dictionary or encyclopedia of puzzling language.

- Use a person's passion or interest as a way to make a connection and start a conversation. Because some individuals will have difficulty moving away from favorite topics (and this is true for all of us at times), using fascinations can help develop a relationship with someone and build trust. Rather than avoiding the subject, try finding new ways to engage the person in the subject. Ask him to find out new information for you. Play a game related to the topic. Take turns sharing trivia on both of your favorite topics (for example, you share a fact about football, and he shares a question about Antarctica).

- Model the communication you want the person to use. If you want to help the person tell jokes or use humor more effectively, then share jokes regularly, read them out of books, and talk about what makes a joke funny. If you want the person to ask her communication partner questions, ask a lot of these questions in your own interactions with that person. Talk about the questions or, better yet, keep a list of them that the two of you can use in your conversations.

4.6. Strategies for Supporting Those Without Reliable Communication

Too often we focus on what individuals on the spectrum *cannot* do, instead of what they *can* do. All individuals with autism have ways of communicating, even if they do not use spoken words. Does the individual point to objects she wants? Does she use facial expressions to indicate distress, pain, or happiness? Can she use an object or a picture to make a request (such as grabbing her lunchbox when she is ready for lunch)? Can she accurately use a gesture to communicate a need, a want, or a feeling (such as clapping hands when she wants to hear music)? Realize that students without reliable verbal communication often communicate with behaviors, sounds, gestures, and movements and that your task as a good communication partner is to honor the communication that already exists before trying to create new means and methods.

Following are more suggestions for communicating better with those on the spectrum who do not have reliable communication:

- Interpret the best you can and respond accordingly. Some individuals may communicate excitement by jumping up and down or engaging in other repetitive movements. They may show appreciation or desire to connect using touch, proximity, or by simply pacing near another person. They might express frustration by pacing, screaming, or crouching on the floor. Do your best to interpret this communication and respond respectfully to it in any way that seems appropriate (saying, for example, "You seem happy to see me. I am so excited to see you too. I'm glad I could make it to the party.").

- Assume that the person understands what you are saying. We may not always know exactly how much a nonverbal individual understands, but certainly the most responsible way of doing business is to assume the individual is comprehending and is interested in socializing and learning.

- Talk and share. Be sure to converse with people without reliable speech. Just because someone can't speak or uses a lot of echoed speech does not mean he does not understand the communication of others. Too often the only words directed at these individuals are directions, simple questions, and, sadly, reprimands.

- Speaking louder won't help a person with autism listen better, so it is best to use a natural and respectful tone of voice.

- Talk to the person in an age-appropriate manner. Even if someone cannot participate in the give-and-take of a conversation, it is respectful and kind to share stories, jokes, simple small talk, and any information a person of his age group might find interesting.

- Don't assume that all the individual's communication is intentional. Some individuals do not have command of their bodies and behaviors, and may therefore say and do things they do not intend to say or do. Because of significant movement problems and learning differences, some on the spectrum may have moments when their speech does not work well for them. For instance, they may say no when they mean yes or ever ask for their shoes when they actually want a drink of water.

- Watch and learn together. For those with significant disabilities, a team approach may work best to help in understanding communication. Family members, therapists, and others might sit together and view a few videotapes of the person to examine all the ways the individual makes requests and choices, responds to humor, communicates love and affection, demonstrates knowledge, and interacts with others. For instance, as the team watches a tape of the student getting ready for school, the child's mother might point out how she taps her head to ask for her hat, vocalizes "buh" to ask for her favorite book, or touches the faces of people she likes.

- If you find it challenging to have a complex conversation with someone who does not speak, look for materials that can help you generate conversation. You might read aloud from the newspaper, comment about what is on television, look through photo albums and chat about the pictures, involve the person in a multipartner conversation so there are many ideas to share and build from, or simply use familiar objects (such as a new augmentative communication device) as catalysts for small talk.

- "Listen" to augmentative and alternative communication (AAC) users. The communication act is incredibly dynamic when an AAC system is being used, so the AAC user may have a difficult time interrupting, interjecting, or even initiating a conversation if the communication partner is not sensitive to communicative behaviors beyond speech. For example, an AAC user may begin a conversation by pointing to a word on a board. Such an initiation will be missed if the communication partner does not attend visually to the AAC user and look for signs that the AAC user wants to join the conversation (by placing a hand on a communication board or shifting the body, for example). A communication partner should also be aware of and open to changes in the pace of conversation. Many times a communication partner will cut the AAC user off in midsentence because he thinks he knows what is going to be typed or signed next, or he may grow impatient with the AAC user's attempts to communicate and prematurely end a conversation.

- If the individual on the spectrum uses AAC (such as sign language or picture symbols), then others in her life should use them too. If a learner with autism uses a picture board to indicate choices, the teacher might ask all students to use a picture board for choices at some point in the day, thereby teaching another method of expression and communication to all. If a child is learning gestures and signs to communicate, the entire family should not only learn these gestures and signs, but use them regularly in their own communication with the child with autism and with each other.

4.7. Strategies for Encouraging and Supporting Social Relationships

Realize that friendships cannot be created by outsiders. As teachers, parents, friends, or support workers, we can only encourage, give plenty of opportunities for building social relationships and interaction, and help students learn how to give and get support. Following are just a few strategies for encouraging and supporting social relationships with people on the spectrum:

- Give individuals with autism opportunities to interact with others of their age group and others with shared interests. Look for summer camps, after-school activities, clubs, and community groups that might be good matches for the individual's needs and interests. Depending on the person's age, try to provide her with opportunities to just hang out (with either peer or adult support) in places where same-age peers will be congregating, including gyms, parks, libraries, movie theaters, malls, after-school recreation centers (such as the YMCA and Boys & Girls Clubs), and even restaurants and coffee shops frequented by teens.

- Create conditions that will help relationships begin and flourish. Creating these conditions might mean making adaptations to the environment (such as allowing a student who struggles to socialize and interact in a busy and bustling cafeteria to eat in an adjacent room with a few other students), making changes to activities (such as offering a wider range of activities at the church picnic or summer camp), or allowing students to socialize with just one or two peers at a time in certain instances (such as playing a game of chess during indoor recess instead of playing charades with the whole class).

- Create structures for socializing when none exist. During free times such as recess, students may be much more successful with peers if adults are on the playground teaching and modeling new games and activities. Social workers, counselors, teachers, or paraprofessionals might be recruited for this purpose (see www.peacefulplaygrounds.com for information on offering more structure and building community during recess periods). This same concept can be honored during time with the family. If the aunts, uncles, cousins, and grandparents are coming over for a holiday, the individual with autism may feel more socially successful if there are games or activities to join. Parents may want to set up a craft or simple game for young kids or suggest that older children put on a talent show, put together music-compilations on the computer, make a dessert together, or go for a bike ride.

- Practice games that children play. Small children, for instance, like to play tag, king of the hill, hide and seek, red light–green light, "pretend," and chasing games. Try these games at home or outside of school and help the child learn the necessary competencies.

- Give those with autism a job or enjoyable task to complete during the most difficult social situations. If you know that the child will struggle or feel fearful at a given event, this will be an even more important recommendation. A young child can mix the lemonade at a picnic and be in charge of giving out drinks. An older child can be the DJ, taking requests and selecting music for the different parts of the day. This strategy often allows individuals to interact with others one at a time or at least in smaller groups than they might encounter in the thick of the event.

- Teach some of the skills related to social relationships. Turn taking, for instance, is a necessity for most games and activities. Talk about turn taking, practice it, point out examples of it in television programs and books, make up stories about it, and explicitly teach how it is done. Other skills you may need to teach include greeting people, beginning or ending a conversation, making small talk, sharing materials, respecting personal property, and honoring personal space.

- Some individuals may find it helpful to watch social interactions on video to learn new strategies and identify problem situations. Videos created specifically for the purpose of learning social skills can be used for this purpose. Another option is to watch popular television shows that feature young people involved in solving problems and navigating social terrain—*Saved by the Bell, Dawson's Creek, The Brady Bunch, Hannah Montana,* and *Zoey 101* are all good examples of this type of program.

- Many on the spectrum will find comfort in developing relationships online. Some use the Internet for dating, others for gaming (such as online chess), and still others to connect with people who share the same fascinations (such as Battleship enthusiast groups) and goals (such as weight-loss message boards). While you may also want to encourage relationships beyond cyberspace, these friendships are often very important to people on the spectrum and should be seen and honored as real connections.

4.8. Strategies for Building Social Skills

Building and honing social skills is a life-long job. Small children have to learn how to get along on the playground, join games and activities, and build conversation skills. Older students must cope with cliques, learn to navigate the community, figure out the puzzle of parties and social experiences, and even learn the dating game. In any of these situations, the following strategies may help individuals on the spectrum build social skills and competencies:

- Parents or teachers can encourage proper social skills by regularly playing games or engaging in fun cooperative activities. For instance, while driving on a long trip, a family can play the "compliment game," in which each person in the family gives a compliment, a thank-you, or a thoughtful comment to someone else in the car. A teacher can structure cooperative games where, for instance, students pass a ball around a circle and can speak only when they are holding the ball.

- Go to the movies. Videotape the individual in a social situation and watch it with her afterwards. Ask her to evaluate the things she does well and to identify any difficulties if she can. Then gently point out any social skills that might be improved.

- Give the individual opportunities to improve social skills with role play. You can practice using scripts at first and then move to partially scripted scenes and finally to having the individual ad-lib as you try different scenes and situations.

- Practice makes perfect. Teach specific behaviors and responses the individual can use across situations and contexts. For instance, you might explicitly provide guidelines for dealing with a bully, for coping when feeling upset, or for getting help when feeling confused.

- Read all about it. Using age-appropriate books and videos, you can teach good manners and give the individual a rule-based system for learning social skills. There are many great manners guides available for children and adolescents, including the following titles:

  365 Manners Kids Should Know: Games, Activities, and Other Fun Ways to Help Children Learn Etiquette, by S. Eberly (Three Rivers Press, 2001)

  How to Behave and Why, by M. Leaf (Universe, 2002)

  How Rude! The Teenager's Guide to Good Manners, Proper Behavior, and Not Grossing People Out, by A. J. Packer (Free Spirit, 1997)

- Some on the spectrum need help learning to pay attention to moods and expressions and to correctly label feelings. Draw or use pictures of faces with different expressions and ask him to label related feelings. Once he is able to label some feelings, help him identify situations when he might feel these emotions himself.

- Don't assume that individuals on the spectrum will be able to "read between the lines." You may need to explicitly teach the person to read body language, to ask for clarification or look for help when confused. You may also need to teach about specific situations such as how to tell which events are accidental (as opposed to purposeful).

- Teach and rehearse appropriate voice levels across settings. For instance, the individual may not easily be able to figure out that at the dinner table you speak loud enough for everyone to hear you, but not so loud that you are yelling. If he or she needs help assessing and using the correct voice level, recording the person's voice on video or audio in different contexts can help. These tapes can be played for the person while a parent or teacher gives tips on how to make necessary adjustments.

4.9. Addressing Movement Differences

People on the autism spectrum often have difficulty start-ing, stopping, combining, executing, and switching movements (Donnellan & Leary, 1995). They may use a lot of excessive move-ment (such as hand flapping or rocking), speak very slowly or very quickly, struggle with fine motor tasks, or find transitioning from movement to movement or activity to activity very difficult. Following are some ways to address these and other movement problems:

- Consider whether or not you need to do something about the movement or behavior. If the child flaps her hands when she gets excited, this is not necessarily something you need to correct. If she mutters to herself when she is stressed out, this might be a coping strategy that you want to allow and possibly encourage. Repetitive behavior in many instances serves a purpose for the individual with autism. It may be relaxing for some. Others may find movements help them sit for longer periods or simply feel more physically "organized" or even more safe. Too often professionals will seek to "extinguish" these behaviors without understanding that they may be taking away something important or useful.

- Vigorous exercise, frequent breaks, and opportunities for movement are all helpful for individuals on the spectrum. All of these should be woven into the individual's life as needed, keeping in mind that it is better to offer them preventively than wait until the person is in distress. For instance, in a school setting, students with significant movement problems should be given regularly scheduled walking or sensory breaks. Families can also incorporate these types of breaks into community outings. For instance, you might schedule one or two bathroom breaks in the middle of church services each week so that your child does not need to sit for periods longer than fifteen or twenty minutes at a time. Chores or errands can also be opportunities for needed movement. A person on the spectrum might be given the task of passing out materials before a lesson (especially if he has been sitting for a long period of time).

- Watch to see when and where specific behaviors emerge. This way you will find out more about their function and potentially be able to add in other supports to meet the individual's needs. For instance, if the individual seems to grind her teeth in order to block out loud noises, you might be able to provide headphones to give extra support. If she bangs her head when there is a lot of commotion, help her create a sanctuary in her home. If he bites his wrists when he doesn't have needed information, try to provide some type of augmentative and alternative communication to help him ask questions.

- If a repetitive movement or quirk is very distracting or dangerous to others (or to the person on the spectrum), you might look for a behavior substitute. Simply asking or telling the person to stop—or, worse yet, forcing her to stop (by grabbing her hands or putting your arms around her, for instance)—may backfire and even cause an increase in the behaviors. If a student is making loud noises, for instance, you might suggest she listen to some music. If a person is rocking very vigorously, invite her to bounce on a trampoline or run on a treadmill.

- Another way to deal with movement problems that are distracting to others or seem to cause problems for the person on the spectrum (such as screaming) is to create times and spaces for the individual to engage in these behaviors without correction, reprimand, or redirection. After school, for example, the child may be allowed to go to his room and scream for a certain period of time.

- One movement problem that is often misunderstood is "inappropriate" laughter. Some on the spectrum laugh at unusual times and may even do so during very serious moments. Be aware that this laughter may be a signal of distress or panic. For instance, if a student is biting his own wrist and laughing strangely as he being confronted by the principal, he may actually be devastated but unable to show the appropriate feelings. Provide reassurance and comfort, not reprimands, in these situations.

- Provide visuals. Some people can become "unstuck" when they have visual supports to help them. A person who is hesitating or resisting a transition from the house to the car might be shown a picture of the car or given a card that reads, "Time to get in the car." A person who is on the floor and seems unwilling or unable to get up might be given a note that reads, "Let's stand up together."

- Use auditory cues. If a particular transition is difficult, add a song or even rhythmic language. For instance, if a child resists starting his end-of-the-day routine, play a short song to help him initiate the process. Or, instead of music, try another sound or auditory cue. A person who is becoming agitated might be provided with an audio recording of his grandfather reciting a favorite poem or joke.

- Teach visualization. If a person freezes at the bottom of a stairwell, ask her to imagine herself climbing a mountain and talk her through each flight by providing additional details about the mountain scenery or the climbing equipment. If she cannot speak easily under certain circumstances, have her imagine that someone she feels comfortable around (her mother, perhaps) is in the room. Encourage the person to then create their own images.

- Introduce cognitive strategies. Teach the person to use mantras such as "I can do this" or "Just take one step at a time." Show him how to set a small goal such as, "I am going to get into the pool for just three minutes."

- Try physical support. If a person is trying to speak but is stuttering excessively, putting your hand lightly on her wrist may make a difference. If the individual is walking with a gait that is very unsteady, walking next to her or even holding her arm may help.

- Self-injurious behavior may be seen when the student is experiencing extreme anxiety or frustration. In these instances, it is usually best to calmly and gently try to provide comfort and coax the individual to reduce or stop the behavior. You might present him with a preferred object or start talking about a favorite topic. You could also begin singing a favorite song or give suggestions about being calm in a rhythmic voice or a whisper.

4.10. Addressing Sensory Issues: Visual

The blinking and flashing of electronics, sunshine, fluorescent lights, cluttered and chaotic spaces, and certain colors can all be visually challenging for people on the spectrum. Following are some ways to address visual sensitivity:

- In environments where the individual spends a lot of time (such as the bedroom or the classroom), look around to see whether you can reduce visual clutter. Look at the arrangement of materials. Are things easy to find? Is the space confusing, or is it clearly organized?

- Scanning a room and navigating a space can be difficult for some. Look for ways in which spaces can be organized to help the individual with autism work, live, and play independently. If coordinated outfits are placed in bins with day-of-the-week labels on them, the individual will find it easier to dress on her own. If craft supplies are separated into categorical bins and containers, children will find it easier to both choose activities and clean up afterwards.

- Certain spaces may also be visually overstimulating. Video arcades, theaters, and some theme restaurants may be a challenge for some on the spectrum, especially if strobe lighting or very bright lights are used.

- Be aware that some computer Web sites can be overstimulating or otherwise problematic for those on the spectrum. This may be especially true of sites with blinking lights, changing images, or lots of bright colors. Look in particular for Web sites that are Bobby-approved, which means they are more accessible to people with disabilities (www.cast.org/products/Bobby). Certain gadgets (such as hand-held computer games) may also have these features.

- Problems with lighting—especially fluorescent lighting—are one of the most common complaints of people on the spectrum. There are many adaptations you can make if lights are problematic. (See Checklist 3.11: Creating a Comfortable Classroom for information and ideas on lighting).

- For those who are particularly sensitive to light, sunglasses may be helpful. Glasses might be worn during recess, car trips, or even indoors where there is fluorescent lighting. A visor or baseball cap can also used for these purposes.

- Keep it in the dark. Assess whether or not you need lights when indoors. If you are the principal meeting with a student on the spectrum, shut off your fluorescents to have that difficult discussion about playground behavior. At home, eat by candlelight or dim the lights if needed.

- Be aware of potential coping strategies. Repetitive behaviors such as rocking, hand flapping, or even the spinning of objects may be signs that the person on the spectrum is overwhelmed in some way. Some people on the spectrum engage in these behaviors as a way to deal with visual sensitivity. If you see this type of behavior, look for potential challenges in the environment and, by all means, if the behavior seems to be helping the person calm down, manage discomfort, or regain focus do not interfere.

4.11. Addressing Sensory Issues: Tactile

Some on the spectrum won't want to use or touch certain materials or textures. These same individuals may find other materials very appealing. As we learn about these differences and preferences, we can use this understanding to support people. Following are some ways to address the tactile issues of people on the spectrum:

- Learn about the likes, dislikes, and aversions of those you love or support. Some children love the feel of glue and water, but won't touch sand. Others may love the feel of sand, but will avoid touching newspapers, foam, or plastic bags.

- Some children and youngsters will find the textures of certain foods either very pleasing or repulsive. A child or young person who has severe problems with a wide range of foods can end up eating a very restricted and even harmful diet. To cope with this constraint, you can try introducing many different foods and encouraging the individual to try them. You can also add calories and nutrients by preparing special shakes and smoothies.

- Some with autism do not like to be touched, do not like to be touched in certain places (such as the back of the head), or can tolerate only certain kinds of touch. To be on the safe side, ask for permission before touching or reaching out to touch person with autism. For example, ask, "Can I shake your hand?" Or if touch is unavoidable, let the person know what will be happening, where you are touching her, and why. For example, "The doctor needs to touch your head and ears now to see if you have an ear infection."

- Issues with touch may be especially challenging when it comes to washing and bathing. Try teaching the individual to wash her own face and hands thoroughly (perhaps by dabbing soap on her forehead, cheeks, and chin and challenging her to clean off the bubbles). You can also use soapy wipes or liquid soaps if the person finds these items more appealing.

- Another major challenge for many on the spectrum is hair care. So many individuals find hair washing and hair brushing uncomfortable and, in some cases, even painful. To avoid struggles, choose a soft hairbrush or give the person several to choose from and let her tell or show you which one is best. You will also want to consider this challenge when styling or cutting hair. If you are a parent, for instance, you will probably want to avoid braids for a child who hates to have her hair touched and may want to minimize accessories in general.

- Shaving is another difficulty. Some adults on the spectrum opt to keep beards and moustaches for this reason. An electric razor might work for some who have this sensitivity.

- Consider different clothing options for individuals who cannot tolerate certain materials or the tags on their garments. Some clothing companies make items such as underwear and shirts without tags. Others specialize in creating soft clothing for people with sensory needs. And if you find a shirt or a pair of pants the individual really likes, consider buying several!

- A favorite garment of some children and teens is a hooded sweatshirt. It can feel comfy on the head and cause a nice safe sensation; it can also serve as a mini-escape when the world feels too overwhelming.

4.12. Addressing Sensory Issues: Auditory

If you have ever been with a person on the spectrum when an alarm rings or a siren sounds, you may have seen the distress that auditory sensitivity can bring. Following are some ways to address the auditory issues of people on the spectrum:

- Use a calm, quiet voice as much as possible, especially if the individual is upset. Many on the spectrum report that whispers are very comforting.

- Save them from the bell. Alarms, sirens, and bells may all cause stressful reactions in students with auditory sensitivity. When possible, look for ways to avoid exposing the person to these often painful experiences. A teacher, for instance, might allow a student with autism to sit as far away from the bell as possible or use noise-canceling headphones at passing time. A parent might avoid driving past fire stations as much as possible.

- Reduce noise. Add carpeting or carpet remnants. Hang curtains. Put tennis balls or rubber tips on the bottoms of table and chair legs. Look into appliances that have noise reduction features. Place TV sets on stands instead of on the floor. Use central air conditioning rather than window units, if possible. Use lower or quieter settings on appliances. Install insulation around dishwashers, washers, or dryers. Add soundproof windows. Use double drywall on walls facing a noisy street or add thick hedges outside. Install extra layers of asphalt roofing if you live near an airport.

- Keep the volume down. For video games, televisions, computers, and other electronics, use the lowest setting possible.

- Replace the sound. For instance, if a child bristles at the shrill ring of the telephone, change to a model that can play music instead. If the microwave buzzer is too hard on the person's ears, buy a handheld timer that the person can tolerate.

- Block it out. Allow the person to listen to soft music using headsets in noisy or chaotic environments.

- Provide earplugs or headphones. The person will still be able to hear your voice but will not hear as many distractions. If she does not tolerate headphones, don't give up until you have tried a few different types. Some people won't wear large headphones that completely cover their ears, but will wear ear buds. Others won't put anything in their ears, but willingly use headsets with foam ear pieces. Noise-canceling headphones may also be tried.

- Beware of the munchies. Some foods cause auditory problems for people on the spectrum. It may be difficult for some to tolerate the loud crunch of foods like tortilla chips, rice cakes, or even popcorn.

- Be aware that sounds in the environment may be causing behavior problems, so when a person seems to fall apart, explode, or melt down for no apparent reason, assess the possibility of auditory sensitivity. Could he be responding to sounds others cannot detect (such as the sound of other people sucking on candy several feet away)? Could he be responding to sounds we hear but don't perceive as problematic (such as the faint beeping sound of a faraway garbage truck backing up)?

4.13. Addressing Sensory Issues: Olfactory

We certainly cannot control every smell in the environment or predict which smells around us will affect the person with autism. We can, however, arm ourselves with some strategies for helping a person with a sensitive nose and olfactory system. Following are some ways to address this particular sensitivity in people on the spectrum:

- Get feedback from the individual about different smells in the environment. Make it a practice to learn which smells are pleasing and which ones are problematic.
- Skip the aftershave. Many individuals with autism report that perfume and other personal products cause problems. If an individual on the spectrum seems to avoid a particular person or if she will interact with that person only occasionally, consider that she may be reacting to that person's perfume, lotion, hair gel, aftershave, cologne, or shampoo. If the individual is very sensitive to these types of smells, family members and staff should avoid the use of products with heavy scents as much as possible.
- Avoid places and situations that will be too difficult for the person on the spectrum. For some, this may be the coffee shop; for others, it may be gas stations.
- Look for an opening. In places with strong smells (such as a restaurant), those on the spectrum can be seated near the door or a window.
- Give the person a small personal fan. This can be used not only to cool off and keep comfortable temperature-wise, but also to diffuse offensive or overpowering smells.

- Use pleasant scents to replace unpleasant ones. If desired scents can be identified, they might be used to support the individual with autism. For instance, if a child likes the smell of peppermint, then candies or scented lotion can be used to soothe him at difficult times or to counteract another smell that is bothering him.

4.14. Strategies for Teaching and Learning

Whether you are a camp counselor, the grandmother of a child on the spectrum, or a home health worker, you may be responsible for teaching a person on the spectrum something. Following are some helpful teaching and learning strategies that will work whether you are trying to teach someone to use an augmentative communication system, play a game, or wash his face:

- Be positive. Point out what the person is doing right.
- Be patient and calm. Some with autism will need repeated attempts to learn certain new behaviors, tasks, or concepts.
- Look to the learner to set the pace of the lesson or session. Watch for signs of frustration and take breaks when needed.
- As Temple Grandin, a woman with autism, has shared, "Many people with autism are visual thinkers. I think in pictures. I do not think in language. All my thoughts are like videotapes running in my imagination. Pictures are my first language, and words are my second language" (Grandin, 2002, p. 1). Visuals help students feel more safe and organized and make environments feel more secure. They can also help students become more independent as they learn to rely on cues instead of people. If you are trying to teach a child to set the table, for example, it might help to prepare a placemat with an outline of where the plate, fork, spoon, knife, glass, and napkin should be placed. If you are trying to teach a teen to follow a simple recipe, use drawings as well as written directions for each step.
- Talk about your own experiences learning something new or difficult. Even if the individual does not have reliable communication and therefore cannot contribute to the discussion, share your thoughts and experiences and let him

know the challenges we all face in doing and understanding new things.

- Use a soft and steady voice. Voices that are too loud or too excited may be distracting to the individual and, in some cases, hard to decipher.

- Break tasks down into small steps. To teach a child to brush her teeth, it might help to first teach just the retrieving of the toothbrush from the stand. When this step has been mastered, add additional steps.

- When possible, teach experientially. Demonstrate what you want done. Allow the child or young person with autism to try the task with you before you ask him to do it alone.

- Make learning comfortable, stress-free, and, of course, enjoyable whenever possible. Teach by using a student's passions if you can easily embed them. Or create conditions that are pleasing to the individual. For instance, if the youngster likes to spend time curled up in blankets on the couch, this is probably a better place to practice reading than the kitchen table.

- Try, try, and try again. If at once you don't succeed, try again under different circumstances. For instance, you might try teaching the game of catch outside, indoors, with other children, and with energizing music on or off. You can also try using different materials. In the same example of playing catch, you could try the game with a beach ball, a rubber ball, a Koosh ball, a football, or even a preferred object such as a plush toy. Finally, you might try a different teaching partner altogether. If you haven't had success, ask another adult to make an attempt. If dad does not have success, mom might. If mom does not have success, a sibling or peer might.

4.15. Promoting and Teaching Organization

Promoting and teaching organization will help students feel more relaxed, confident, and in control. Further, people on the spectrum who work, learn, and play in organized spaces are learning and adopting skills they can take into adult life. Following are good ways to promote and teach organization for those on the spectrum:

- Model the use of organizing tools such as calendars, to-do lists, daily schedules, and project time lines. As you use these tools, talk about the process. For instance, if you keep a large family calendar in your kitchen, explicitly discuss what you put on it and why. Let the child add stickers for special days or cross off each day as it passes.

- Color-code supplies to make organizing easier. A math notebook and textbook cover can be red, while the materials for science can be green. This principle can translate to home life as well.

- Object outlines can be used to give those with autism a clear idea of what belongs where. For instance, a desk blotter might be created with the outlines of a pencil can, a stapler, and a tape dispenser to help the individual keep the work space organized.

- Label all equipment and materials that belong to the individual with autism, especially those items that travel outside the home. A marker will suffice for things like school bags, balls, or lunch boxes. For papers, folders, books, or simple electronics, print the name and phone number on sheets of address labels and keep them handy. Teach the individual this strategy and help her get in the habit of labeling important possessions.

- Ensure that the individual has all the materials he needs for each class or activity. You might even create different containers for this purpose. At home, for instance, you can create one bag for soccer, one for the library, and one for going to the sitter's house. All materials used for these excursions should be housed in these bags and these bags alone. In school, teachers can create folder systems or even section off a locker in this way.

- Give the individual a small keychain tape recorder so that reminders can be created and saved instantly. Or have her call herself on the phone to leave voice mails that can be retrieved later and serve as an electronic string around the finger.

- Create an IRS reminder system. When we send in our taxes, the IRS doesn't want us to forget payment or necessary documents, so they put a little reminder message on the envelope (such as Did you sign your name? Did you enclose your payment?). This same strategy can be used in the home or in classrooms. A parent might post a sign in the kitchen with the following questions: Do you have your phone? Do you have your wallet? Do you have your homework? Similarly, a teacher might post a sign on his classroom door with reminders for all students: Do you have a pencil? Do you have your assignment?

- Provide checklists to help the individual on the spectrum:
  - Pack for trips
  - Get organized for an outing
  - Gather materials
  - Follow common routines
  - Finish long-term projects
  - Tackle a long-term goal
  - Complete all steps of assignments
  - Keep track of tasks to be done

- Create as clean and orderly a work space as possible. It will be easiest for youngsters with autism to get organized and stay organized if there is a "place for everything and everything in its place." It should be clear to students where supplies are housed, where work should be handed in and stored, and where toys and materials are kept. At home, environments should be similarly structured. Video games, movies, CDs, toys, books and magazines, school supplies, and other often used materials should be kept in clearly labeled containers that can be easily accessed. One key part of organizing is providing appropriate containers and storage space for supplies. If sandals and sneakers are lying all over the bedroom, purchase a hanging shoe organizer for the closet. This is a better storage option than, say, a large laundry basket. If the student's desk is a mess, provide separate containers for writing implements, art supplies, and math tools or outfit a locker with extra hooks, hanging pockets, and bins designated for certain subject areas.

- For supplies that are needed in many environments, it may be helpful to allow students to store these things where they are used. For some students, traveling with too many materials can result in frustration and lots of missing items! If a student does projects in more than one room in the house (the basement and his bedroom, for instance) it is probably better to keep art supplies in both of those places. If a sharpened number-two pencil is required in every class in the high school and the student regularly comes to class without one, consider allowing her to keep a supply pouch in every classroom.

- Teach the individual strategies for getting and staying organized. For instance, work with him to file papers in appropriate folders and bins at the end of each lesson. Do this with him until it becomes a habit.

4.16. Helping Those on the Spectrum Cope with Change

Few on the spectrum would agree with the claim that "change is good." For most with autism or Asperger syndrome, change is scary, frustrating, or at least disappointing. Unfortunately, change cannot always be avoided, but the following suggestions may help those on the spectrum cope a bit better:

- Prepare the individual ahead of time, if possible, by warning him of upcoming changes. It is almost always a mistake to assume that a change will be easier if it is unexpected.

- Use visual as well as verbal explanations of upcoming or sudden changes. Videotapes, photographs, drawings, or maps can all help a parent, teacher, or care provider ready an individual for something novel or unexpected. If a new route must be taken to Aunt Jada's house, a drawing of some of the upcoming landmarks can be offered. If a new person is coming into the individual's life, you could show pictures of the person or even talk to her via the Skype feature on the computer to make the upcoming face-to-face meeting more comfortable.

- Many on the spectrum, especially children, use a visual schedule (an illustrated list of every activity of the day) to manage their time and organize their day. For those with such a tool (or for those with any type of calendar or schedule system), change can be addressed by including the new information in the schedule and by sharing the information in advance.

- Acknowledge that the individual may be stressed the first time she meets new people (such as teachers or babysitters) or visits new places (such as a new school or a new home). Suggest that the person prepare herself for these instances. You might remind her to bring a favorite possession or rehearse how she will act or respond when she is in the new situation.

- Introduce mantras that might be helpful in times of challenge, such as "This too shall pass" or "Just breathe."

- Talk about how *you* deal with change. Give examples of times when you have struggled with change, and share how you dealt with each situation.

- Point out how characters in television shows and movies deal with change and challenges. For instance, you might talk about how Dora the Explorer dealt with having a new baby brother and sister or how a favorite *American Idol* contestant coped with being voted off the show. This approach is especially effective if the characters are from preferred programs. Talk about how the person feels, how he coped with difficulty, and specifically how he behaved in the face of a change or a challenge.

- For some, drama therapy or bibliotherapy may be useful in learning to cope with change. In this method, individuals read or act out stories with specific themes or lessons. Stories about change would be the focus of study in this instance. One of our favorite resources for learning about this approach is a book by Paula Crimmens titled *Drama Therapy and Storymaking in Special Education* (2006).

- Give the person a physical way to experience a transition or change. If a new baby is coming into the family, have the child move some of his old toys into the nursery. If a pet fish dies, let the child bury it in the yard.

4.17. Addressing Challenging Behavior

Many of the other lists in this book will help with preventing and addressing behavior challenges. The items in this list, however, are some of our most tried-and-true tips. Following are some constructive ways to address challenging behavior and difficult moments:

- Be careful about using punishment as a response to challenging behavior. Punishment indicates to the individual that she has done something wrong; it does not, however, help her understand alternatives or appropriate behavior. In most cases, it also fails to teach new skills or competencies.

- Analyze the behavior. Observe. Talk to the person and those who know him well. Consider whether or not the behavior has meaning. Is it intentional? What need, if any, does it serve? Is the person using it to communicate? Is the behavior a symptom of discomfort or pain?

- Those with autism or Asperger syndrome may find it difficult to talk directly about difficulties, especially if they feel they are at risk or in trouble. Try instead talking about the same problem happening to an unspecified friend or tell a story about how a favorite television or cartoon character might handle a similar problem.

- Adapt if possible. Assess the person's environment to see which tasks or activities cause strife and see if these can be avoided or adapted in some way. For instance, if coming in from the playground always leads to protests and tears, try giving the student a leadership role during the transition (such as line leader) or pairing him up with a friend who will keep him company during the transition.

- Teach a skill that may be needed. If the person is acting out because he can't play a game that others are playing, teach the game. If he is frustrated because he wants to play a video but mom is on the phone, teach him to use the DVD player.

- Prepare whenever possible. Many a behavior challenge has sprouted from a schedule change or unexpected event or circumstance (such as a bus arriving late or a substitute teacher). Try to prepare the student for these changes or at least prepare to be comforting and available when such changes arise and no preparation was possible.

- Break it down. Chunking big tasks down into more manageable parts can prevent some difficulties. A child will probably respond better to a request to "pick up ten blocks" than to "clean up the play area."

- Just relax. Teach the person how to bring stress levels down. Introduce meditation, relaxation exercises (such as "tense and release"), visualization, or even yoga. Help the person "go" to these techniques when they are emotionally struggling.

- Ask the person for input. Ask for her ideas for preventing difficult behavior in the future.

4.18. Strategies for Coping in Crisis

When someone is in crisis, the only appropriate response is to help find a way out of it. When a person is coming unglued or already seems unable to regain control, be prepared to provide the most calm, gentle, and generous supports you can. The following are some strategies for helping people on the spectrum cope in crisis:

- Remain as calm as possible. It will be hard for a person in crisis to relax if the people around her are tense or angry or tempers are escalating. If calming down is a challenge, try using deep breathing exercises, counting slowly to ten, or even getting help from someone else nearby who can take over.

- Don't try to teach in crisis. When a person appears to be losing control or is already out of control, it is not an appropriate time to make threats, review what consequences will be, remind the learner of the upcoming punishment, or even teach about what the individual needs to do to avoid such a crisis in the future. The goal during crisis is to get out of the crisis situation.

- Use a low, calm voice or even whisper as you speak. If you raise your voice or use threatening words, the student will most likely react it and the crisis will be in danger of escalating.

- Use reassuring language (such as "How can I help?")—or say nothing at all. Warnings, and ultimatums are not helpful in crisis situations.

- Try walking without talking. Do this not in a punitive way, but rather to communicate solidarity, peace, and calm.

- Do something unusual that the person might not expect and may find comforting. Try singing softly, counting to one hundred, or even dancing to shift the person's attention away from the moment.

- Give the person concrete suggestions for calming down. You might suggest he engage in visualization or try relaxation strategies (such as tensing and releasing the shoulders).

- Provide information. If the person is upset about an unexpected schedule change, for instance (such as early dismissal due to bad weather), try giving as much information as you can about the situation. You might show her the bulletin sent by the superintendent or talk to her about the weather and consequences of weather. It may help to tell her the specific reasons students are being sent home (as, for example, when it's not safe for busses to be on the road after rain freezes).

- Pick up a pencil. If the person doesn't seem able to calm down while you are talking, try writing him a message or drawing images that will help him understand what you want him to do, what is coming next, or what might help him relax.

- Reduce the number and the intensity of demands. If the individual is struggling because the task is too difficult or because there is too much going on at once, move the person to a calmer environment, reduce the requirements of the task, or redirect her to an activity or task that is less stressful.

- Bring the individual items that he might find soothing or comforting. If he has a favorite toy, lucky charm, book, or picture, give him some time and space to use or enjoy it. Someone who loves to draw, for example, might be offered his sketch book.

- If you know the person has a coping strategy that works for her, be sure to use it in crisis. If classic rock music works as a tool for soothing, grab an iPod. If the individual has a favorite book she uses in times of struggle, pull it off the shelf and start reading.

- Consider any medical or physical cause of the behavior. Is the person in pain or experiencing discomfort? Some outbursts—especially those that seem to come out of the blue—may actually be seizure activity. Epilepsy is not uncommon in people with autism and can be difficult to diagnose due to both the communication and sensory differences of those on the spectrum.

5

HELPFUL RESOURCES FOR PARENTS AND TEACHERS

Introduction

Introduction

Looking for a good book on social skills? Want some reliable Web sites to turn to for strategies on schooling, communication, or family issues? Interested in a DVD to help others learn about autism? We can help. In this section we have compiled lists of our favorite DVDs, books, Web sites, organizations, and vendors to help you connect, learn, and find answers.

Our first list consists of recommended DVDs that will be of interest to people on the spectrum, their families, and anyone who cares about, supports, or teaches people on the spectrum. This list is followed by one on recommended books and one on recommended Web sites. To make browsing this chapter easier, we have divided both the book and the Web site sections into the following categories: autism, autobiography and self-advocacy, behavior, communication, families, inclusion, sensory and movement differences, social support, and teaching and learning. Though some of the books and Web sites we have categorized undoubtedly cover more than one of these areas, we have organized them by the primary topic or topics they address.

The list of vendors has similar content, but is organized under only five categories: communication, inclusion, sensory and movement differences, social supports, and teaching and learning. The vendors in this list offer everything from augmentative communication devices to adapted toys.

Finally, we have included a list of ten organizations that can help educators, support workers, and families through outreach, networking, provision of resources, referrals, and national and regional conferences. The list represents just a fraction of the groups that are available to serve families, schools, and communities in learning about and sharing resources for individuals on the spectrum. We hope you can use our list as a starting point for exploring what is available in your city, state, or country.

Obviously there are far more quality resources than we could share in these pages, so we want to clearly communicate that we don't consider these lists to be all-inclusive. More resources become available for families, schools, and communities every day, and we are constantly finding new favorites to use ourselves and recommend to others. We feel confident, however, that the ones we suggest in this section will be a solid starting point for learning more about autism and Asperger syndrome and for getting needed information.

5.1. Recommended Videos

Autism: The Musical
Tricia Regan, Bunim-Murray Productions (2007).
www.autismthemusical.com

> Winner of two primetime Emmys, *Autism: The Musical*
> follows five children over the course of six months. Director
> Tricia Regan captures the reality of their family lives and
> observes how performing in a musical production gives the
> kids a comfort zone and an opportunity to express their uni-
> queness.

Autism Is a World
Geraldine Wurzburg, State of the Art (2004).
www.stateart.com/works.php?workId=27

> *Autism Is a World* is a short-subject documentary film written
> by Sue Rubin, a woman with autism. The film, a glimpse
> into Rubin's life and mind, was produced and directed by
> Gerardine Wurzburg and coproduced by CNN cable network.
> It was nominated in 2005 for an Academy Award for Best
> Documentary Short Subject.

Including Samuel
Dan Habib, (2007).
www.includingsamuel.com

> This film does not concern autism in particular, but it will be
> of interest to many families and teachers. The film is built on
> the efforts of the director and his family to include Samuel,
> age eight, in all facets of school and community. *Including
> Samuel* also profiles four other families and features interviews
> with dozens of teachers, young people, parents, and disability
> rights experts.

Inside the Edge: A Journey to Using Speech Through Typing
J. Gamble, Syracuse University (2002).
www.inclusioninstitutes.org/index.cfm?catID=51
> Written and narrated by a young man named Jamie Burke, this video shows his progress as he moves from typed communication to reading what he has typed and eventually to speaking spontaneously without the use of typed words.

Mozart and the Whale
Peter Naess, Big City Pictures (2005).
> *Mozart and the Whale* is inspired by the love story of Jerry and Mary Newport, both people with Asperger syndrome, who married, divorced, and married again.

"We Thought You'd Never Ask": Voices of People with Autism
Paula Kluth, John Hussman, Beret Strong, and John Tweedy; The Hussman Foundation (2009).
www.landlockedfilms.com/index.htm or www.paulakluth.com
> A short video featuring six adults with autism answering questions such as, What is autism? What is good or helpful about autism? and What is support?

5.2. Recommended Books

Autism

Ariel, C., & Naseef, R. (2006). *Voices from the spectrum: Parents, grandparents, siblings, people with autism, and professionals share their wisdom.* Philadelphia: Jessica Kingsley.

Attwood, T. (2008). *The complete guide to Asperger's syndrome.* Philadelphia: Jessica Kingsley.

Biklen, D. (2005). *Autism and the myth of the person alone.* New York: NYU Press.

Parish, R. (2008). *Embracing autism: Connecting and communicating with children in the autism spectrum.* San Francisco: Jossey-Bass.

Shore, S. (Ed.). (2004). *Ask and tell: Self-advocacy and disclosure for people on the autism spectrum.* Philadelphia: Jessica Kingsley.

Williams, D. (1996). *Autism: An inside-out approach.* Philadelphia: Jessica Kingsley.

Zysk, V., & Notbohm, E. (2004). *1001 Great ideas for teaching and raising children with autism spectrum disorders.* Arlington, TX: Future Horizons.

Autobiography

Barron, J., & Barron, S. (1992). *There's a boy in here.* New York: Simon & Schuster.

Blackman, L. (2001). *Lucy's story: Autism and other adventures.* Philadelphia: Jessica Kingsley.

Gerland, G. (1997). *A real person: Life on the outside.* London: Souvenir Press.

Grandin, T. (2006). *Thinking in pictures: my life with autism, Expanded edition.* New York: Vintage Books.

Grandin, T. (2008). *The way I see it: A personal look at autism and Asperger's syndrome.* Arlington, TX: Future Horizons.

Grandin, T., & Scariano, M. (1996). *Emergence: Labeled autistic.* New York: Warner Books.

Hall, K. (2001). *Asperger syndrome, the universe and everything.* Philadelphia: Jessica Kingsley.

Jackson, L. (2002). *Freaks, geeks, and Asperger syndrome: A user guide to adolescence.* Philadelphia: Jessica Kingsley.

Lawson, W. (1998). *Life behind glass.* Philadelphia: Jessica Kingsley.

Mukhopadhyay, T. R. (2003). *The mind tree: A miraculous child breaks the silence of autism.* New York: Arcade.

O'Neill, J. L. (1999). *Through the eyes of aliens: A book about autistic people.* Philadelphia: Jessica Kingsley.

Prince-Hughes, D. (2004). *Songs of the gorilla nation: My journey through autism.* New York: Harmony Books.

Robison, J. E. (2007). *Look me in the eye: My life with Asperger's.* New York: Crown.

Shore, S. (2003). *Beyond the wall: Personal experiences with autism and Asperger syndrome* Second edition. Shawnee Mission, KS: Autism Asperger.

Tammet, D. (2007). *Born on a blue day: Inside the extraordinary mind of an autistic savant.* New York: Free Press.

Tammet, D. (2009). *Embracing the wide sky: A tour across the horizons of the mind.* New York: Free Press.

Willey, L. H. (1999). *Pretending to be normal.* Philadelphia: Jessica Kingsley.

Williams, D. (1992). *Nobody nowhere: The extraordinary autobiography of an autistic.* New York: Avon.

Williams, D. (1994). *Somebody, somewhere: Breaking free from the world of autism.* New York: Times Books.

Behavior

Baker, J. (2008). *No more meltdowns: Positive strategies for managing and preventing out-of-control behavior.* Arlington, TX: Future Horizons.

Bailey, B. (2001). *Conscious discipline: Seven basic skills for brain smart classroom management.* Oviedo, FL: Loving Guidance.

Dunn, K., & Curtis, M. (2004). *The incredible 5-point scale: Assisting students with autism spectrum disorders in understanding social interactions and controlling their emotional responses.* Shawnee Mission, KS: Autism Asperger.

Jones, A. (1998). *104 activities that build: Self-esteem, teamwork, communication, anger management, self-discovery, coping skills.* Richland, WA: Rec Room.

Kluth, P., & Schwarz, P. (2008). *Just give him the whale! 20 ways to use fascinations, areas of expertise, and strengths to support students with autism.* Baltimore: Paul H. Brookes.

Lovett, H. (1995). *Learning to listen.* Baltimore: Paul H. Brookes.

Smith Myles, B., & Southwick, J. (2005). *Asperger syndrome and difficult moments: Practical solutions for tantrums, rage, and meltdowns.* Shawnee Mission, KS: Autism Asperger.

Communication

Beukelman, D. R., & Mirenda, P. (2006). *Augmentative and alternative communication: Supporting children and adults with complex communication needs.* Baltimore: Paul H. Brookes.

Biklen, D., & Cardinal, D. (Eds.). (1997). *Contested words, contested science: Unraveling the facilitated communication controversy.* New York: Teachers College Press.

Downing, J. (2005). *Teaching communication skills to students with severe disabilities* (2nd ed.). Baltimore: Paul H. Brookes.

Flodin, M. (2004). *Signing illustrated: The complete learning guide* (Rev. ed.). New York: Perigee Trade.

Gray, C. (1994). *Comic strip conversations.* Arlington, TX: Future Horizons.

Greenspan, G. (2006). *Engaging autism: Helping children relate, communicate, and think with the DIR Floortime Approach.* New York: Da Capo Lifelong Books.

Mirenda, P., & Iacono, T. (Eds.). (2008). *Autism spectrum disorders and AAC (augmentative and alternative communication)* Baltimore: Paul H. Brookes.

Mukhopadhyay, T. (2008). *How can I talk if my lips don't move? Inside my autistic mind.* New York: Arcade.

Families

Barron, J., & Barron, S. (1992). *There's a boy in here.* New York: Simon & Schuster.

Collins, P. (2005). *Not even wrong: A father's journey into the lost history of autism.* New York: Bloomsbury.

Dowling, C., Nicoll, N., & Thomas, B. (Eds.). (2006). *A different kind of perfect: Writings by parents on raising a child with special needs.* Boston: Trumpeter.

Fling, E. (2000). *Eating an artichoke: A mother's perspective on Asperger syndrome.* Philadelphia: Jessica Kingsley.

Ginsberg, D. (2002). *Raising Blaze.* New York: Harper Collins.

Hughes, R. (2003). *Running with Walker.* Philadelphia: Jessica Kingsley.

Kephart, B. (1998). *A slant of sun.* New York: Norton.

LaSalle, B. (2004). *Finding Ben.* New York: McGraw-Hill.

Mont, D. (2002). *A different kind of boy.* Philadelphia: Jessica Kingsley.

Sakai, K. (2005). *Finding our way: Practical solutions for creating supportive home and community for the Asperger syndrome family.* Shawnee Mission, KS: Autism Asperger.

Savarese, R. (2007). *Reasonable people: A memoir of autism and adoption—on the meaning of family and the politics of neurological difference.* New York: Other Press.

Waites, J., & Swinbourne, H. (2001). *Smiling at the shadows: A mother's journey through heartache and joy.* New York: Harper Collins.

Willey, L. H. (2001). *Asperger syndrome in the family: Redefining normal.* Philadelphia: Jessica Kingsley.

Inclusion

Downing, J. (2002). *Including students with severe and multiple disabilities in typical classrooms.* Baltimore: Paul H. Brookes.

Falvey, M. (2005). *Believe in my child with special needs! Helping children achieve their potential in school.* Baltimore: Paul H. Brookes.

Johnson, M. D., & Corden, S. H. (2004). *Beyond words: The successful inclusion of a child with autism.* Knoxville, TN: Merry Pace Press.

Kinney, J., & Fischer, D. (2001). *Co-teaching students with autism.* Verona, WI: IEP Resources.

Kluth, P. (2003). *"You're going to love this kid": Teaching students with autism in the inclusive classroom.* Baltimore: Paul H. Brookes.

Sapon-Shevin, M. (1999). *Because we can change the world: A practical guide to building cooperative, inclusive classroom communities.* Boston: Allyn & Bacon.

Sapon-Shevin, M. (2007). *Widening the circle.* Boston: Beacon Press.

Schwarz, P. (2006). *From disability to possibility.* Portsmouth, NH: Heinemann.

Schwarz, P., & Kluth, P. (2007). *You're welcome: 30 innovative ideas for the inclusive classroom.* Portsmouth, NH: Heinemann.

Sensory and Movement Differences

Biel, L., & Peske, N. (2005). *Raising a sensory smart child: The definitive handbook for helping your child with sensory integration issues.* New York: Penguin.

Donnellan, A., & Leary, M. (1995). *Movement differences and diversity in autism/mental retardation: Appreciating and accommodating people with communication and behavior challenges.* Madison, WI: DRI Press.

Gillingham, G. (1995). *Autism: Handle with care.* Edmonton, Canada: Tacit.

Heller, S. (2003). *Too loud, too bright, too fast, too tight: What to do if you are sensory defensive in an overstimulating world.* New York: Quill.

Kranowitz, C. (2006). *The out-of-sync child: Recognizing and coping with sensory processing disorder* (Rev. ed.). New York: Perigee.

Kranowitz, C. (2006). *The out-of-sync child has fun: Activities for kids with sensory processing disorder (Rev. ed.).* New York: Perigee.

Smith-Myles, B., Cook, K., Miller, N., Rinner, L., & Robbins, L. (2000). *Asperger syndrome and sensory issues: Practical solutions for making sense of the world.* Shawnee Mission, KS: Autism Asperger.

Social Support

Baker, J. (2003). *The social skills picture book: Teaching play, emotion, and communication to children with autism.* Arlington, TX: Future Horizons.

Baker, J. (2006). *Preparing for life: The complete guide for transitioning to adulthood for those with autism and Asperger's syndrome.* Arlington, TX: Future Horizons.

Grandin, T., & Barron, S. (2005). *The unwritten rules of social relationships: Decoding social mysteries through the unique perspectives of autism.* Arlington, TX: Future Horizons.

Gray, C. (2000). *The new social story book* (Illus. ed.). Arlington, TX: Future Horizons.

Henault, I., & Attwood, T. (2005). *Asperger's syndrome and sexuality: From adolescence through adulthood.* Philadelphia: Jessica Kingsley.

Moor, J. (2008). *Playing, laughing and learning with children on the autism spectrum: A practical resource of play ideas for parents and carers.* Philadelphia: Jessica Kingsley.

Tashie, C., Shapiro-Barnard, S., & Rossetti, Z. (2006). *Seeing the charade: What we need to do and undo to make friendships happen.* Nottingham, UK: Inclusive Solutions.

Teaching and Learning

Arwood, E. L., & Kaulitz, C. (2007). *Learning with a visual brain in an auditory world: Visual language strategies for individuals with autism spectrum disorders.* Shawnee Mission, KS: Autism Asperger.

Bender, W. N. (2009). *Differentiating math instruction: Strategies that work for K–8 classrooms.* Thousand Oaks, CA: Corwin Press.

Buchen, I. (2004). *Parents' guide to student success.* Lanham, MD: Scarecrow Education.

Cohen, M. J., & Sloan, D. L. (2007). *Visual supports for people with autism: A guide for parents and professionals.* Bethesda, MD: Woodbine House.

Dyrbjerg, P., & Vedel, M. (2007). *Everyday education: Visual support for children with autism.* Philadelphia: Jessica Kingsley.

Erickson, K., & Koppenhaver, D. (2007). *Children with disabilities: Reading and writing the four-blocks way.*® Greensboro, NC: Carson-Dellosa.

Feldman, J. (1995). *Transition time: Let's do something different.* Beltsville, MD: Gryphon House.

Gregory, G. (2005). *Differentiating instruction with style: Aligning teacher and learner intelligences for maximum achievement.* Thousand Oaks, CA: Corwin Press.

Kluth, P., & Chandler-Olcott, K. (2008). *"A land we can share": Teaching literacy to students with autism.* Baltimore: Paul H. Brookes.

Palmer, A. (2005). *Realizing the college dream with autism or Asperger syndrome: A parent's guide to student success.* Philadelphia: Jessica Kingsley.

Savner, J. L., & Myles, B. S. (2000). *Making visual supports work in the home and community: Strategies for individuals with autism and Asperger syndrome.* Shawnee Mission, KS: Autism Asperger.

Smith, S. (2000). *The power of the arts: Creative strategies for teaching exceptional learners*. Baltimore: Paul H. Brookes.

Udvari-Solner, A., & Kluth, P. (2008). *Joyful learning: Active and collaborative learning in the inclusive classroom*. Thousand Oaks, CA: Corwin Press.

5.3. Recommended Web Sites

Autism

The Autism Acceptance Project
www.taaproject.com

> The Autism Acceptance Project aims to disseminate a different and positive view about autism to the public "in order to create tolerance and acceptance in the community." Their Web site is rich and varied, offering articles, artwork, stories written by people with autism, conference information, and a blog written by EstéAe Klar-Wolfond, the mother of a child on the spectrum.

Autistics.org
www.autistics.org

> This Web site is filled with resources for learning about autism and Asperger syndrome through the eyes of those on the spectrum. It contains many short essays and offers discussion forums and blogspace for those with autism or related labels.

Celebrating Autistic Parents
cap.autistics.org

> A site designed to show the abilities and needs of parents on the spectrum and to highlight the experiences of this population.

Neurodiversity.com
www.neurodiversity.com

> This portal site was set up by a parent of a child on the spectrum to "help reduce the suffering of autistic children and adults, who often face extraordinary challenges in many domains of life, challenges made more difficult by others' unrealistic expectations and demands."

Positively Autism

www.positivelyautism.com

>*Positively Autism* is a free e-magazine celebrating the "sunny side of the spectrum."

Autism Self-Advocates

Brian King

www.imanaspie.com

>This is the Web site of an adult on the spectrum who is also a licensed social worker. King specializes in helping children and adults with autism labels. His Web site will be interesting to anyone on the spectrum, as well as those who love or support people on the spectrum.

Wendy Lawson

www.mugsy.org/wendy

>Wendy Lawson is the author of several books, a poet, and a presenter. Her Web site includes dozens of her papers, talks, and interviews.

Temple Grandin

www.templegrandin.com

>Grandin, perhaps the best-known woman with autism in the world, has a Web site featuring past interviews and articles and a list of her upcoming speaking engagements.

Lars Perner

www.delightfulreflections.blogspot.com

>In his delightful blog Perner comments on not only the autism spectrum but also a range of topics including marketing, consumer behavior, and education.

John Elder Robison

www.jerobison.blogspot.com

> This blog is updated regularly, is often illustrated with photos, and features a wide range of topics such as what it means to be smart, personal fascinations, and learning from other people on the spectrum.

Stephen Shore

www.autismasperger.net

> One of the best speakers around in the area of autism and Asperger syndrome, Shore offers materials that are straightforward and often humorous. As a person with autism, a teacher, and a professor, he offers insight from many valuable perspectives. Visit this site to learn more about his life, experiences, and many books.

Sarah Stup

www.sarahstup.com

> This is a very well-crafted Web site featuring the poetry and essays of this young artist.

Daniel Tammet

www.optimnem.co.uk

> Tammet, author of the wildly popular book *Born on a Blue Day,* has a Web site that not only provides information about his life, art, and writings, but also offers classes and teaching materials for learning Spanish and French.

Donna Williams

www.donnawilliams.net

> The author of four autobiographies and four textbooks, Williams was one of the first to share her story of life with autism with the world. Her site includes links to her blog, podcasts, and videos on YouTube.

Behavior

A Compassionate Heart

www.acompassionateheart.com

> A Compassionate Heart offers support to individuals with challenging behavior that stems from trauma, mental illness, or transition. The Web site contains a collection of articles, useful links, workshop schedules, an event calendar, blogs, forums, and a directory of national resource centers.

Crafting Gentleness

www.craftinggentleness.org

> The Crafting Gentleness Web site is essentially an invitation to consider the practice of gentleness in personal life, work, and community. The essay on "helpful thinking" is especially relevant, we believe, for those teaching and supporting individuals on the spectrum.

Person-Centered Planning Education Site

www.ilr.cornell.edu/edi/pcp

> This Web site is focused on person-centered planning, which enables people with disabilities to make choices and to have agency in their own lives. The site offers an overview of the planning process and a self-study course on this topic, readings, and helpful links.

Imagine Consulting (David Pitonyak's Web site)

www.dimagine.com

> Pitonyak's site features sensitive and useful articles on supporting students with significant disabilities and plenty of information on behavior.

Gentle Teaching

www.gentleteaching.com

> Gentle Teaching is a site focused on fostering compassion, gentleness, and sensitive support in our schools. It is

especially helpful for those working with students with significant behavior challenges.

Communication

Core Communication Partners
www.darlenehanson.com

> Crafted by speech and language pathologist Darlene Hanson, this site offers a great newsletter, several helpful forms, and links to vendors and other resources. Topics addressed on the site range from building communication competencies to respecting your communication partner to learning about new technology.

Everyone Communicates
www.everyonecommunicates.org

> This site is dedicated to people "who are still waiting for a means to communicate more effectively." A particular commitment of the Everyone Communicates Web site is to present the writings and stories of individuals who communicate by using augmentative and alternative communication methods.

The Inclusion Institutes and the Facilitated Communication Institute
www.inclusioninstitutes.org/fci

> This group conducts research, public education, training, and scholarly seminars. The site contains dozens of short articles written by people with autism on subjects ranging from life with autism to communication needs to social relationships.

Simplified Technology (Linda Burkhart's Web site)
www.lburkhart.com

> Visit this site for several great make-it-yourself ideas. Burkhart provides clear directions on how to make your own talking switch, for instance. Many helpful handouts are offered as well, with special focus on students on the spectrum.

Families

Alyson Beytien

www.alysonbeytien.com

> Beytien is a nationally known popular speaker, as well as a mother of three children with autism. Her Web site features information about her consulting services along with hundreds of links to related sites and resources.

JaynaGirl Web site

http://jaynagirl.cwd-cragin.com

> This site was created by the father of a daughter on the spectrum and offers information not only on autism but also on ADHD and Tourette syndrome.

Kristi Sakai

www.kristisakai.net

> This mother, author, and speaker has three children on the spectrum. Her blog is the centerpiece of her Web site and is well worth regular visits. You can also download some of her presentations and view her speaking schedule here.

Lianne Holliday Willey

www.aspie.com

> Holliday Willey is not only a gifted writer and speaker, but also an advocate for adults and young people on the spectrum. As the parent of an "Aspie" and an individual on the spectrum herself, Willey offers words and ideas from a lifetime of experience.

Inclusion

Broadreach Training and Resources

www.normemma.com

> This Web site is created by two veteran consultants and educators in the inclusive schooling movement, Norman Kunc and Emma Van der Klift. Visit the site for audio interviews

on inclusive schooling, scholarly articles, and information on professional development.

Creating Ideal Lives
www.ideallives.com

A parent-centered Web site with resources on inclusion and family life. Sign up for free sixty-second e-messages.

Inclusion: School as a Caring Community
www.ualberta.ca/~jpdasddc/inclusion/schoolcaring/intro.htm

This fantastic Web site is filled with short essays written by general and special educators. Teachers share tips on everything from creating curricular adaptations to building an inclusive school to supporting students with behavior struggles. It can be especially helpful for secondary education teachers.

Inclusive Solutions
www.inclusive-solutions.com

Every teacher will find something helpful, interesting, or inspiring on this Web site. It is packed with short articles, video clips, illustrations, photographs, training ideas, and recommendations for books, speakers, and workshops. There are also many elaborate examples of using mind mapping and graphic facilitation to plan inclusive experiences.

Patrick Schwarz's Web site
www.patrickschwarz.com

Schwarz's site contains a definition of inclusive schooling, recommendations for "literacy for all," and a list of useful links.

Paula Kluth's Web site
www.paulakluth.com

My Web site offers dozens free of articles on autism, inclusive schools, teaching and learning, and literacy instruction that can be used for staff development purposes or simply to inspire new practices in schools.

Respect Diversity Web site

www.respectdiversity.org

The Respect Diversity Foundation, a tax-exempt nonprofit organization, was created "to help people of all ages successfully live, learn and work in our increasingly diverse society." This distinctive group and Web site serve as a virtual gathering place for any group or individual interested in social justice, inclusion, and respect for human differences.

Sensory and Movement Differences

BrainGym International

www.braingym.org

BrainGym is a worldwide network dedicated to enhancing living and learning through movement. The mission of this group and the Web site is to help children and adults learn faster and more easily, be more focused and organized, and overcome challenges.

Miss Kelly OT (Kelly Redd's Web site)

www.misskellyot.com

Visit this Web site for tips on hand strengthening, recommendations for appropriate toys and games, and ideas for addressing writing problems.

The Out-of-Sync Child

www.out-of-sync-child.com

Like the popular book of the same name, this Web site has information on supporting students with sensory challenges and a great resource directory. Information on Carol Stock Kranowitz's books can also be found here.

Sensory Fun

www.sensoryfun.com

Learn about sensory issues from a mother's perspective. On this site you will find one family's story of addressing sensory differences along with fun games for kids.

Teaching and Learning

The Access Center

www.k8accesscenter.org/index.php

The Access Center is a national technical assistance center funded by the U.S. Department of Education's Office of Special Education Programs. Their mission is to improve educational outcomes for elementary and middle school students with disabilities.

CAST

www.cast.org

CAST is a nonprofit organization that works to expand learning opportunities for all individuals, especially those with disabilities, through the research and development of innovative, technology-based educational resources and strategies.

Power of Two

www.powerof2.org

This Web site, sponsored by the Office of Special Education Programs, is specifically designed to help schools move their collaborative models forward. Its Web-based training modules are especially helpful.

Read, Write, Think

www.readwritethink.org

NCTE and IRA have collaborated to create a Web site highlighting the highest-quality practices and resources in reading and language arts instruction through Internet-based content. It is chock full of lessons, teaching materials, and activities for students of all ages, and it is all free.

TeachersFirst
http://teachersfirst.com/matrix.cfm
The Teachers First Web site offers thousands of ideas for teaching nearly every subject area and for addressing the needs of students with disabilities. Browse the special education links as well as the various subject areas to get ideas for your students.

Social Skills and Support

Dennis Debbaudt's Autism Risk and Safety Management
http://autismriskmanagement.com/links.html
This unique and important Web site should be in the favorites folder of every teacher, police officer, and parent. The site has publications, links, safety products to review, and information for both people with autism and for those who love and support them.

Pacer Center's Kids Against Bullying
www.pacerkidsagainstbullying.org
A unique site that empowers kids to build community, support one another, and create safer school environments.

Social Skills Training
www.socialskillstraining.org
This site highlights strategies for teaching social skills to children and adolescents.

Teaching Resources from the Desk of Laura Candler
www.lauracandler.com/socialsk.htm
Though not geared toward students with autism specifically, this site offers a nice step-by-step guide to teaching social skills in schools. Also check out Candler's tips for creating a caring classroom.

5.4. Recommended Vendors

Communication

Ablenet
www.ablenetinc.com
(800) 322–0956 or (612) 379–0956

Communication devices, switches, and several computer-access products (such as adapted keyboards) can all be found on this site.

Attainment Company
www.attainmentcompany.com
(800) 327–4269

Attainment offers a wide range of products to support communication, including single message talkers, multiple message talkers, communication books, and talking photo albums.

Don Johnston, Inc.
www.donjohnston.com
(800) 999–4660 or (847) 740–0749

This company, familiar to most teachers of students with disabilities, sells technology that supports reading, writing, phonics, and communication.

Dynavox Systems LLC
www.dynavoxsys.com
(800) 344–1778

Dynavox Systems offers many products for individuals with speech, language, and learning challenges. Some of the most popular include the DynaVox, Dynamite, DynaWrite, and Lightwriter, devices.

Frame Technologies
www.frame-tech.com
(414) 869–2979

On this site you will find several voice-output communication aids (such as Voice-in-a Box and TalkPad) ranging in complexity and price.

Mayer-Johnson Co.
www.mayer-johnson.com
(800) 588–4548

This is a must-visit site for communication software, symbol sets, display materials, books, and videos. All the Boardmaker materials are available here as well.

Inclusive Schooling

Disability Is Natural
www.disabilityisnatural.com

Disability is Natural promotes positive new images and ideas related to disability and difference. Several short, free articles are available, as well as products related to person-first language and inclusive education.

Inclusion Press
www.inclusion.com

Visit this site for inspirational stories and inclusion-related DVDs, posters, and books.

The Nth Degree
www.thenthdegree.com

This is one of our favorite sites. It contains great articles on disability rights and fun products too, including bumper stickers, T-shirts, and pins.

Sensory and Movement Differences

Pocket Full of Therapy

www.pfot.com

> You will find everything an occupational therapist needs at this site, including adapted scissors, slant boards, seat cushions, games, touch windows, and software.

Sensory Comfort

www.sensorycomfort.com

> Sensory Comfort offers products for children and adults who have sensory processing differences (such as seamless socks and tactile towels).

Therapy Works, Inc.

www.alertprogram.com

> Visit this site to learn about a program that supports children, teachers, parents, and therapists in choosing appropriate strategies to change or maintain states of alertness. Kids learn "how their engine runs" and are introduced to strategies that help them manage challenges.

Weighted Wearables

www.weightedwearables.com

> As the name suggests, this site features weighted adaptive products (such as "lap landers" and "wonder vests") that facilitate proprioceptive feedback and increase postural stability and attention span.

Social Supports

The Gray Center for Social Learning and Understanding
www.thegraycenter.org

Those at the Gray Center work to "improve social under-standing on both sides of the social equation," helping individuals on the spectrum communicate and interact more successfully with the people with whom they live and work. Products in the store include books and videos on Carol Gray's Social Stories™ method.

Model Me Kids
www.modelmekids.com

This site features video modeling DVDs that teach social skills.

Teaching and Learning

Creative Communicating
www.creativecommunicating.com
(435) 645–7737

Creative Communicating offers the Storytime series of products, teacher resource manuals, videos, puppets, software programs, adaptive equipment, and online courses.

Enabling Devices
www.enablingdevices.com
(800) 832–8697

Shop this site for a wide variety of innovative adapted toys and switches (such as switch-activated stuffed toys and gumball switches).

IntelliTools

www.intellitools.com

(800) 899–6687

Several assistive technology products are available from this company, including the popular IntelliKeys, an alternate keyboard for anyone with physical, visual, or cognitive disabilities who struggles to use a standard keyboard.

Slater Software, Inc.

www.slatersoftware.com

(877) 306–6968

You can find picture writing software and applications (such as Read and Tell) at the Slater Software site. Download lesson plans free of charge.

Turning Point Therapy and Technology, Inc.

www.turningpointtechnology.com

(877) 608–9812

This virtual shop carries everything from big display calculators to environmental controls to low-tech communication boards and books.

5.5. Recommended Organizations

The ARC
www.thearc.org

> The Arc is the world's largest community-based organization of and for people with intellectual and developmental disabilities. It provides an array of services and support for families and individuals.

Autism National Committee
www.autcom.org

> Autism National Committee is dedicated to social justice for all citizens with autism through a shared vision and a commitment to positive approaches. This group does not provide any direct services, but does sponsor regular conferences, create original publications, and partner with other groups to sponsor human rights activities. Their Web site features links, conference information, and many articles and position papers on topics ranging from abuse and the use of aversives to inclusive education.

Autism Network International
http://ani.autistics.org

> Autism Network International is an autistic-run self-help and advocacy organization for autistic people. The Web site offers several articles written by those with autism and Asperger syndrome and contains links to dozens of personal Web sites created by people on the spectrum. The group also sponsors AUTREAT, a retreat-style conference run by autistic people, for autistic people and their friends.

Autism Society of America
www.autism-society.org

> Autism Society of America is a grassroots organization that aims to increase public awareness about the day-to-day issues

faced by people on the spectrum, advocate for appropriate services for individuals across the lifespan, and provide the latest information regarding treatment, education, research, and advocacy. Their Web site offers ample information for families, caregivers, and others. You will find a tip of the day, information on how to connect with people in your local community, and autism news. Materials are available in Spanish as well.

Autism Speaks
www.autismspeaks.org/index.php

Autism Speaks is a group dedicated to funding research and raising public awareness about autism. Their Web site offers several downloadable resources. See, in particular, the School Community Tool Kit, with articles and videos (including a clip of Kluth discussing inclusive schools) related to including students with autism. The kit features specific tips for bus drivers, custodians, and other school staff members.

CAUSE
www.causeonline.org

Citizens Alliance to Uphold Special Education (CAUSE) aims to protect and advocate for the educational rights of students with disabilities.

Closing the Gap
www.closingthegap.com

Closing the Gap provides parents and educators with the information and training needed to locate, compare, and implement assistive technology. Through their annual international conference, magazine, and Web site, they provide the latest information and training available for individuals with disabilities and those who work with them.

PEAK Parent Center

www.peakparent.org

> PEAK's mission is to provide training, information, and technical assistance for all disability conditions and equip families with strategies to advocate successfully for their children. PEAK assists families and others through services like its telephone hotline, workshops, conferences, and Web site.

PACER Center, Inc.

www.pacer.org

> PACER Center's mission is to expand opportunities and enhance the quality of life of children and young adults with disabilities and of their families. Their work is specifically focused on "parents helping parents."

TASH

www.tash.org

> TASH is an international membership association leading the way to inclusive communities through research, education, and advocacy. In general, TASH members are people with disabilities, family members, fellow citizens, advocates, and professionals.

References

Crimmens, P. (2006). *Drama therapy and storymaking in special education*. Philadelphia: Jessica Kinglsey.

Donnellan, A. (1984). The criterion of the least dangerous assumption. *Behavioral Disorders*, 9, 141–150.

Donnellan, A., & Leary, M. (1995). *Movement differences and diversity in autism/mental retardation: Appreciating and accommodating people with communication and behavior challenges*. Madison, WI: DRI Press.

Durand, V. M. (2008). *Helping parents with challenging children*. New York: Oxford University Press.

Grandin, T. (2002). Teaching tips for children and adults with autism. Retrieved March 15, 2009, from www.autism.org/temple/tips.html.

Harmin, M. (1995). Inspire active learning. Edwardsville, IL: Inspiring Strategy Institute.

Hippler, K., & Klicpera, C. (2004). A retrospective analysis of the clinical case records of "autistic psychopaths" diagnosed by Hans Asperger and his team at the University Children's Hospital, Vienna. In U. Frith & E. Hill (Eds.), *Autism: Mind and brain*. Oxford, U.K.: Oxford University Press.

Individuals with Disabilities Education act (IDEA) Data. Number of children served under IDEA Part B by disability and age group, 2006 [retrieved January, 2009]. Available at: https://www.ideadata.org/arc_toc8.asp#partbcc.

Mercier, C., Mottron, L., & Belleville, S. (2000). Psychosocial study on restricted interest in high-functioning persons with pervasive developmental disorders. *Autism, 4,* 406–425.

Leary, M. R., & Hill, D. A. (1996). Moving on: Autism and movement disturbance. *Mental Retardation, 34*(1), 39–53.

Robison, J. E. (2007). *Look me in the eye: My life with Asperger's.* New York: Crown.

Sellin, B. (1995). *I don't want to be inside me anymore.* New York: BasicBooks.

Shore, S., & Willey, L. H. (2004). *Ask and tell: Self-advocacy and disclosure for people on the autism spectrum.* Shawnee Mission, KS: Autism Asperger.

Williams, D. (1996). *Autism: An inside-out approach.* Philadelphia: Jessica Kingsley.

Index